Oxford Modern Britain   SERIES EDITOR: JOHN SCOTT

Religion in Modern Britain

The *Oxford Modern Britain* series comprises authoritative introductory books on all aspects of the social structure of modern Britain. Lively and accessible, the books will be the first point of reference for anyone interested in the state of contemporary Britain. They will be invaluable to those taking courses in the social sciences.

ALSO PUBLISHED IN THIS SERIES

Age and Generation in Modern Britain
Jane Pilcher

Race and Ethnicity in Modern Britain
David Mason

Youth and Employment in Modern Britain
Kenneth Roberts

FORTHCOMING TITLES

Women and Work in Modern Britain
Rosemary Crompton

Kinship in Modern Britain
Graham Allan

Voting Behaviour in Modern Britain
Anthony Heath

Health and Healthcare in Modern Britain
Joan Busfield

Oxford Modern Britain

Religion in Modern Britain

Steve Bruce

OXFORD UNIVERSITY PRESS
1995

Oxford University Press, Walton Street, Oxford OX2 6DP

Oxford New York
Athens Auckland Bangkok Bombay
Calcutta Cape Town Dar es Salaam Delhi
Florence Hong Kong Istanbul Karachi
Kuala Lumpur Madras Madrid Melbourne
Mexico City Nairobi Paris Singapore
Taipei Tokyo Toronto

and associated companies in
Berlin Ibadan

Oxford is a trade mark of Oxford University Press

Published in the United States
by Oxford University Press Inc., New York

British Library Cataloguing in Publication Data
Data available

Library of Congress Cataloging in Publication Data
Data available
ISBN 0-19-878090-7
ISBN 0-19-878091-5 (Pbk)

10 9 8 7 6 5 4 3 2 1

Set by Hope Services (Abingdon) Ltd.
Printed in Great Britain
on acid-free paper by
Bookcraft (Bath) Ltd.
Midsomer Norton, Avon

Foreword

The Oxford Modern Britain series is designed to fill a major gap in the available sociological sources on the contemporary world. Each book will provide a comprehensive and authoritative overview of major issues for students at all levels. They are written by acknowledged experts in their fields, and should be standard sources for many years to come.

Each book focuses on contemporary Britain, but the relevant historical background is always included, and a comparative context is provided. No society can be studied in isolation from other societies and the globalized context of the contemporary world, but a detailed understanding of a particular society can both broaden and deepen sociological understanding. These books will be exemplars of empirical study and theoretical understanding.

Books in the series are intended to present information and ideas in a lively and accessible way. They will meet a real need for source books in a wide range of specialized courses, in 'Modern Britain' and 'Comparative Sociology' courses, and in integrated introductory courses. They have been written with the newcomer and general reader in mind, and they meet the genuine need in the informed public for accurate and up-to-date discussion and sources.

John Scott
Series Editor

Preface

A short book about religion in modern Britain has to be selective and the selection is bound to be challenged. A few words about my intentions may allay some criticism. First, the geography implied in the title needs to be qualified. The book is primarily concerned with England, Scotland, and Wales; that is, with Great Britain. Where appropriate, it also deals with Northern Ireland; that, and the nature of the state, means that sometimes the unit of analysis is the United Kingdom. Finally, in the historical sections, I sometimes refer to the island of Ireland and hence to the British Isles. In common parlance, the terms 'Britain', 'United Kingdom', and 'British Isles' are often used promiscuously but I have tried to be accurate. Secondly, I have had to assume that most readers will know little or nothing of the beliefs and practices of the various religions described, even those in which they have nominally been raised. There seems little point in talking about how many Jews or Hindus there are in Britain without saying something about the core beliefs of Judaism or Hinduism and the core beliefs even of Christianity will be mysterious to many readers. My potted descriptions will, no doubt, be judged as shallow and misleading by some adherents. I can ask only that those who know far more about the specific faiths described here bear in mind that they are a very small part of the intended audience and tolerate my simplifications. That ethnic minority religions and various new religions will be less familiar to readers than Christianity is one reason why they have been given more space than their size warrants.

As a general orienting principle, I have been more concerned with the public and behavioural elements of religion than with internal spiritual states. Partly this is a necessary accommodation with the methodological problem of studying the inner religious life, which is notoriously hard to access and meaningfully to describe (though I do attempt in parts of the second chapter to work out what goes on in people's minds). Partly it is a consequence of believing that the social interactions of groups of believers, and the structural relations of such groups and the institutions and culture of the surrounding society, if they do not entirely determine, do have considerable impact on internal spiritual states. Or, to put it another way, this is a social scientist's account of religion in modern Britain.

If religious adherents may feel that this book gives too much priority to the agenda of the social scientist, social scientists may feel that it is insufficiently analytical and theoretical. My defence against that charge is to note that this book has a big brother, provisionally entitled *From Cathedrals to Cults: Religion in the Modern World*, which was completed before this was written and which should be published by Oxford University Press in 1995. Some of the descriptive material used here appears in that longer and more overtly sociological work, where it is complemented by comparisons with other societies and illuminated by a much more detailed exposition of my explanatory frame. Those readers who find unsatisfying the attempt to couple the organizational typology of church, sect, denomination, and cult to an evolutionary account of religious change or the concluding defence of the secularization thesis, for example, are referred to the more nuanced treatments to be found in the longer book. In particular, those who suppose that the vitality of religion in the United States poses a fundamental challenge to the secularization approach are advised to stay their criticisms until they have had a chance to read my lengthy treatment of US exceptionalism in *Cathedrals*.

So that the flow of this brief book is not disrupted by relentless citing of sources, only direct quotations in the text have identified origins. The Further Reading sections at the end of each chapter give some detailed guidance on what sources have led me to my conclusions. Again, I would refer the reader who wants more information to consult the extensively annotated *Cathedrals*.

Though I hope it is obvious from the text, I have tried to avoid making theological judgements. Which, if any, of the religions treated here is 'true' is no business of the social scientist, who should always aspire to value neutrality, even if that state is at times difficult to attain.

What do I mean by 'religion'? Social scientists have two very different ways of defining religion. Functional definitions identify it in terms of what it *does*: for example, providing solutions to 'ultimate problems', or answering fundamental questions of the human condition. Substantive definitions identify religion in terms of what it *is*: for example, beliefs and actions which assume the existence of supernatural beings or powers.

Both kinds of definitions pose problems. Functional definitions may count as religious things which do not on the face of it look terribly religious and which their adherents regard as secular: for example, secular therapies or socio-political ideologies. Further, functional definitions have been difficult to use consistently. What is an 'ultimate' problem and ultimate in whose mind are questions that are not easily resolved.

Proponents of such an approach often revert to examining beliefs and institutions which are religious in the more obvious substantive sense. The phenomena they describe seem at times to have little to do with issues of 'ultimacy'. Further, to define religion in terms of social or psychological functions is to beg what is often the most interesting question: just what functions does this or that religion perform in this or that setting? Moreover, given that human beings will always have questions which remain unanswered or problems which continue to raise issues of humanity's existential condition, functional definitions rather prejudge one of the questions most often asked about religion: is it possible for a society to operate without a religion?

Finally, while there are good reasons to want to explore the similarities between religions and other beliefs, and between institutions that perform similar functions, calling them all religions gains us very little except some arguable theoretical baggage and a loss of analytical clarity. One of my main interests is the exploration of the uses to which religion is put. Far from making the study of the 'functions' of religion easier, functional definitions of the phenomenon make it impossible by tautologically mixing into the designation of religion precisely those features of it which we want to establish empirically.

There are also difficulties with substantive definitions. They may be closer to the understanding of the average Westerner, but, when we seek to unpack the notion of 'superhuman' or 'supernatural', we find difficulties with some non-Western or traditional cultures. Where people daily commune with the spirits of their ancestors or take steps to avoid ubiquitous witchcraft, it may not be easy to discriminate the natural from the supernatural in the minds of those concerned.

However, a definition that fits with broad contemporary common-sense reflection on the matter is not a bad place to start. Moreover, the utility of a definition must in the end depend upon the success of the explanations in which it is employed. That is, the purpose of a definition is to bring together analytically similar phenomena, aspects of which we believe we can explain in the same terms. I define religion substantively because this allows me to formulate a number of theories which I believe have considerable explanatory scope. Religion, then, consists of beliefs, actions, and institutions which assume the existence of supernatural entities with powers of action, or impersonal powers or processes possessed of moral purpose. Such a formulation seems to encompass what ordinary people mean when they talk of religion and includes those belief systems such as the more philosophical strands of Hinduism and Buddhism.

Acknowledgements

One way or another, a large number of people and organizations played a significant part in the production of this volume and I would like to acknowledge my debts by briefly mentioning them. Tim Barton of Oxford University Press bought me dinner and commissioned the book. A grant from the Nuffield Foundation allowed me to employ Sandra McIsaac to analyse the data from the 1991 British Social Attitudes Survey and I am extremely grateful to it and to her. Social and Community Planning Research and the Economic and Social Research Council's Data Archive at the University of Essex kindly supplied the original data, and the staff of the University of Aberdeen's Computing Centre were helpful in assisting us with the practicalities of data transfer. As always, OUP's copy-editor Hilary Walford patiently improved my prose.

Dr Paul Heelas of the Department of Religious Studies, University of Lancaster, kindly commented on the material in Chapter Four, and many long conversations with him have much improved my thinking about new religious movements and the New Age. Ahmed Andrews, a postgraduate student and himself a British convert to Islam, stimulated my interest in ethnic minority religion and usefully commented on Chapter Three. But as always my greatest intellectual debt is to the late Roy Wallis, who, in a sadly brief career, produced more original thinking in the sociology of religion than I ever will. Those who know the literature will recognize the debt that Chapter Four owes to Roy's work. Had he lived, this book would have been co-written with him and it would have been all the better for that.

Finally I would like to acknowledge the forbearance of my wife and record my gratitude to her parents, who helped mind our children and restored our house after the ravages of builders. Had they not relieved me of those burdens, this book would have taken a lot longer to write. Hence I dedicate it to Andrew and Jean Duff.

Contents

List of Figures and Tables

Figures

Tables

Chapter One

The Past

This book is concerned with the present state of religion in Britain, but our sense of where we are now and where we might be going is improved if we have a notion of where we have been. A study of the churches does not exhaust 'religion'—many of the more interesting questions about our attitudes to the supernatural are raised by what goes on outside the formal structures of institutional religion—but a brief account of the history of the churches will introduce the major players and arguments within British religion, and a clear image of what religion used to be like will allow us to appreciate what is novel about our own society.

Summarizing the history of five centuries of religion in the four countries that make up the United Kingdom requires some organizing principle. In this introduction, I will concentrate on changes in the ways that churches viewed their mission, and their relations with the state and the common people. Along with the potted history, I will introduce a vocabulary which allows us to use the terms *church*, *sect*, *denomination*, and *cult* in a systematic and neutral manner to describe the general direction of change. I will argue that, as our economy and society became more 'modern', so the church and sect forms of religion were replaced by the denomination. The last fifty years have seen a further shift, with denominations declining and the cultic form of religion becoming common.

The Church and the Sect

Churches aimed to be co-extensive with their societies. They were *inclusive*, in that they offered their ministries to all members of the society (even to those who were unwilling to accept them!). They were closely aligned with the secular social order, fitted into its hierarchy of power and status, and identified more closely with the comfortable classes than with the poor and deprived. When churches were wealthy bodies with extensive powers and lands, their leaders possessed the prerogatives and influence of secular princes and nobles. The clergy were a separate order or 'estate', living a distinctive form of life (for example, by being celibate). Although the clergy were expected to be religious virtuosi, the church made relatively few demands on the common people beyond periodic attendance, financial support, and verbal commitment to its creed.

At the highest levels of its organization, the medieval church was linked to either supra-national entities such as the Holy Roman Empire or to the emerging nation-state, but it entered the lives of ordinary people through the cathedral and through the parish church's ties to the local community. No important social event went unblessed by the church. People were christened, married, and buried by the church. That the clergy were almost the only learned or even literate men in any community reinforced their leading position in local life, and often the church's buildings were the only place the majority of people ever gathered.

In pre-modern societies, religion was not a particularly personal matter. Christendom was made up of Christian societies rather than societies of Christians. The professional clergy performed a prescribed, often calendrical, diet of rituals for the benefit of the people, and not just for a self-selecting group of committed 'members' who took a strong personal interest in the rituals (although there were many such people). The rota of 'offices', spoken and sung in the great cathedrals and humble parish churches, was thought to be effective in glorifying God and meeting his requirements, even if very few lay people attended when they were performed or understood much of what went on when they did. Most church buildings were unheated and had no seating for the congregation, and the offices were spoken in Latin, often by a priest who had his back to the congregation. It is, then, perhaps surprising that the laity ever attended to observe activities which were very much 'mysteries' to them, but many attended regularly and most people attended the most important services.

The notion that the church's professionals could glorify God independently of the involvement of the bulk of the population seems thoroughly foreign to our very individualistic culture. It rested on the implicit assumption that religious merit could be transferred from the religiously observant to those who were less so. Thus people paid to have masses said after their deaths in the hope that the piety of those so paid would speed the sinner's soul to heaven.

This does not mean that our ancestors were not religious people. They were certainly superstitious and, though the more intellectual clergy may have had misgivings, the church generally was happy to link its religion to the wider culture of superstition. Saints and their associated shrines were held to offer powerful remedies for this or that ailment. Discontented wives offered a bag of oats to the statue of St Wilgerfort in the hope of being rid of their husbands. Pregnant women used holy relics to reduce labour pains. Saints protected people and cattle and visited plagues on enemies. 'In 1543, when a storm burst over Canterbury, the inhabitants ran to church for holy water to sprinkle on their houses so as to drive away the evil spirits in the air and to protect their property from lightening.'[1] The common people also had a decent grasp of what were then regarded as the fundamentals of the faith.

The lay parishioners were bound to know by heart the Lord's prayer, the Hail Mary, and to be able to make the sign of the cross. They were to attend Mass on Sundays and great feast days, and to come regularly to communion and confession, for which purpose the priest was to explain to them the Ten Commandments, the three theological and four cardinal virtues, the seven deadly sins and the seven works of mercy. They were also to pay their tithes, bring their babies for baptism (or in emergency baptize them themselves, using the proper formula), and marry at the church door in the sight and hearing of witnesses.[2]

From time to time the church would face dissent or revolt. People would protest against ecclesiastical pomp and wealth or would seek to live out a more radical form of the faith. Those who could not be contained within the church—for example, as a religious order—broke away to form 'sects'. As they often challenged the state as much as the church, they were met with repression. For this, if for no other reason, sects were normally small.

In the church form of religion, there are few or no membership tests and entry qualifications. Though promises that the infant will be taught what is required are usually sought from parents or guardians at the point of baptism, entry into the people of God is by birth. One is not normally born into a sect but becomes a member through choice. The sectarian subjects himself to a demanding moral regime; his commitment and moral standing are rigorously tested before he is allowed to become a full member. Such groups often appeal more to the poor than to the comfortable because they focus on the 'end-times' themes of the Christian tradition: the imminent return of Christ (or the second 'advent') and the coming Millennium (the thousand years' reign of righteousness when the first will be last). Such Adventist doctrines are subversive, as is the rejection of a professional clergy in favour of a democratic priesthood of all believers.

Most divisions in British Christianity have their origins in the Reformation, which can be dated from 1517, when the German priest Martin Luther first issued his catalogue of complaints against the medieval church. The Reformation was far more than a theological dispute. It gave voice to simmering social, political, and economic tensions, and, in so doing, amplified them, and produced massive changes in the societies of western Europe. Most of those features of our world which we think of as distinctly 'modern' have their origins in the Reformation.

Why Luther argued as he did and the consequences of the movement he inspired may well be different matters and it is the second which concerns me. I will concentrate on the subtle and far-reaching implications of the Reformation arguments, rather than on the specific issues which then concerned the protagonists. Two key themes were individualism (in rights and responsibilities) and egalitarianism. Luther, Calvin, Zwingli, and others objected to the idea that religious merit could be transferred and to the religious division of labour it allowed. Individuals had to be responsible for their own souls. But if ordinary people were to be pressed to master their own religious fates, then they had to be able to know what God required of them, and that meant the demystification and simplification of religion. In particular, it meant the translation of the Bible into the vernacular, so that the laity could understand God's word when it was read to them. It meant the end of the priesthood as a special class of people who mediated between God and the laity. Had the Reformers shared the Chinese Communist fondness for slogans, two of their most popular would have been 'Every man his own priest' and 'The priesthood of all believers'. A professionally trained and highly skilled clergy might be useful but it was no longer necessary. In the eyes of God all people were equal.

The other great change was in promoting ethical consistency. Precisely because it embraced the whole society and not just a small group of especially pious people, the medieval church had evolved a system that fully recognized human frailty. We all sinned, but by confessing our sins and repenting of them, and by accepting the penances prescribed by the church, we could periodically regain the state of purity. This system had become corrupted by the gradual relaxation of the requirement for a genuine change of heart. If people could live a life of sin and, by leaving money to the church in their wills, arrange for others to do some religious work that would cleanse their souls, then there was no incentive for people to behave ethically and morally or to pay much attention to the requirements to obey and glorify God. So the Protestants rejected the idea that the clergy had the power to 'absolve' people of their sins and stressed the need for every person to pay systematic and constant attention to the state of his or her soul.

The doctrines of the Reformation were slow to become embedded in the culture of western Europe, but their ramifications were deep and wide. By stressing the rights and responsibilities of the individual and the equality of all in the eyes of God, the Reformers inadvertently undermined the hierarchical vision of society as a pyramid that under-pinned feudalism and they laid the foundations for democracy. Though this was even further from their minds, the Reformers also fragmented Christendom. Although the intention had been to reform *the* church, the consequence of allowing that everyone could discern the will of God and denying that there could in this world be any single authorita-tive source of religious truth (there was, of course, the Holy Spirit, but it failed to prevent disputes and divisions) was the break-up of Christi-anity into a series of competing organizations, each claiming a mono-poly of the truth. We thus have the foundations of cultural pluralism.

To summarize, the pre-modern Christian world was dominated by the *church* type of religion. With the Reformation came the flourishing of *sects*. As they proliferated and as some of them grew to supersede the churches, the state had to change its attitude towards religious confor-mity. Fission created a plurality of organizations, and the divisions of the people of God meant that, even though religious dogmatists wanted to see dissenters prodded into the 'true' church with bayonets, the price of enforcing conformity to the state religion was too high for a modern democratic state. The consequence, quite undesired by most of those who brought it about, was religious toleration and the rise of the secu-lar state.

The shift from church to a plurality of legally equal sects was not easy or even. In England there was an abrupt and partial reformation when Henry VIII, for reasons far more connected with politics than religion, declared an official 'reformation' and severed the links between England and Rome, but Henry's church remained the official state church and retained many of the features of its predecessor. The theo-logical justification for a hierarchy of spiritual wisdom and piety was the idea that Christ passed his powers to the apostle Peter, who then passed them to every successive Bishop of Rome or 'Pope', who in turn delegated those powers to all clergy who were properly ordained. When an ordained priest performed the mass, the bread became the flesh and sinews of Christ. When anyone else did it, the bread remained bread. Priests could forgive sins on God's behalf because Christ's magic had been passed down to them. The break with Rome undermined the Church of England's claims to be part of the 'apostolic succession', as it was known, but it retained the hierarchical structure of archbishops, bishops, deans, and priests.

The Reformation arguments simmered on within the state church and influenced the great political upheavals of revolutions and changes of monarchs. Control of the state and of the church alternated between groups who were more and less 'Protestant', with periodic defections and expulsions. To this day the Church of England or Episcopalian Church (so-called because *episcopos* is the Greek for bishop) is an uneasy coalition of Protestants and Catholics, and in the 1990s the tensions have again been exposed over the ordination of women. Having lost that battle, a number of prominent Anglicans defected to Rome.

The Reformation reached deeper into the religious life of Scotland, where the national church abandoned episcopacy. All full members of a congregation elected a number of *presbyters*, who in turn selected their minister and sent their representatives to the General Assembly, the governing body of the Church. None the less, it remained the legally established state church of Scotland, deriving its income from land and from what amounted to a general tax. Periodically British monarchs, frightened of the revolutionary precedent of an organization that allowed ordinary people to decide things, tried to reimpose an episcopal structure. James VI put it bluntly when he said: 'No Bishop: No King!' Periodically, too, enthusiastic Protestants defected or were expelled and formed dissenting sects.

Waves of religious dissent from the English church came with social and political upheavals. The Civil War period in the middle of the seventeenth century produced the Quakers, the Baptists, and the Congregationalists. But the biggest blow to the idea of a national parish-based state structure came a century later. Methodism can be dated from 1739, the year that John Wesley, a cleric in the Church of England, began his revival preaching. Concerned by what he saw as the spiritually moribund condition of the Church, Wesley revived the classic Protestant doctrine of 'justification by faith'—all that was needed to be saved was to believe that God sacrificed his only son, Jesus Christ, as a full atonement for our sins—and he presented it in an arrestingly popular manner. While many Anglican clergy of the time read out turgid and argumentative sermons, Wesley extemporized and preached to the hearts of his listeners, stressing the evils of hell and damnation and the benefits of salvation. His was a call to religious action and to moral and ethical behaviour, and many people responded.

At first Wesley and his followers worked within the Church of England but bishop after bishop banned the Methodists from church pulpits. They took to preaching in the open air and in public halls and in houses, which further offended the bishops, who thought that religion was something for the hierarchically organized church to deliver in tightly controlled settings. Worse, the Methodists were willing to let people who had not been ordained preach and gave important roles to lay people and to lay women. The result was that they were expelled from the Church of England and developed into a distinct sect or, more exactly, a number of sects and grew rapidly. By 1767 there were 23,000 Methodists. By the end of the century there were almost 100,000. By 1850 there were over 500,000 and in 1900 there were 770,000.

In its social philosophy and impact, Methodism was very different from the earlier sects of the Civil War era. The Ranters, the Levellers, and the Fifth Monarchy Men believed that they lived in the end times and that the Millennium was imminent, to be brought about partly by their own efforts in destroying the established social and religious order. They also wanted political rather than personal change. In contrast, the Methodists offered salvation, not to a society, but to individuals. In so far as they challenged the dominant social arrangements, they did so by attacking the moral standards of individual members of the gentry and by encouraging individual changes of heart. One lady flounced out of a meeting and announced she would never sit and be told her soul was as black as that of a working man! The manifest social problems of the newly urbanizing society would be cured by people becoming moral and ethical in their behaviour and then practising philanthropy.

One powerful obstacle to religious innovation was social and political pressure: in the feudal world, the masses did and believed what they were told. The power of the lord (and his agents) was such that he was able to define the whole ethos and world-view of his people. That is, they really were his people. Methodism spread fastest among those sections of the population that were most free to determine their own beliefs: independent small farmers with tenure in Lancashire and the north of England; tradesmen and craftsmen living in what were called 'free' (as opposed to estate) villages; and the new working class of the towns and cities. Where the Church of England was well organized and funded, with conscientious vicars and a well-organized network of lay workers to involve people in the church, the Methodists had a thin time. Where the vicar took his stipend and went to live in Italy, paying an ill-educated curate a fraction of the income to do the job for him, defections were greater.

Like all 'religions of the oppressed', the new puritanical religion of Methodism offered a critique of the rich that was comforting to the meek, whose lack of any inheritance in this life could be offset by the promise of inheriting the world in the next. As Christ says in the New Testament, it is easier for a camel to pass through the eye of a needle than it is for a rich man to enter the kingdom of heaven. Puritanism also turned present privations into an asset. Not being able to afford to drink alcohol, eat rich foods, dress in flashy clothes, and gamble is a loss; you are short of something that others have. Adopt a faith that says all these things are an impediment to salvation and you may be deprived in the eyes of the world but in the eyes of God you are especially blessed. But Methodism not only reconciled people to their deprived circumstances; it also offered a way out. The converted Methodist stopped drinking, smoking, gambling, and womanizing and became a better worker. He became trusted and so earned more. Because the movement was led and organized by lay people and was democratic in structure, it gave unprecedented opportunities for ordinary people to take charge of a part of their lives and thus gave them the sense that they could affect their own destinies. It also gave opportunities to lead and to organize and it encouraged literacy and public speaking.

Although Methodism was thoroughly individualistic in that it presented both salvation and self-improvement as tasks for the individual rather than for the community and made social change dependent on individual reform, it also offered a cure for the alienation and anomie of the new urban mass society because it provided a strong fellowship for the converted. It is little exaggeration to say that the Methodists (and other dissenters of this period) invented a new social form: the voluntary association. In creating such popular church-related activities as Sunday schools, temperance bands, choral societies, and boys clubs, they also made the template for secular variants. Out of the dissenting culture came penny savings banks, mutual insurance societies, educational associations, sports clubs, trade unions, and political parties.

The Denomination

To return to our basic patterns, increasing religious toleration allowed sects to grow and recruit a following, largely free from civil and political disabilities. Thus the Christian world in the early modern era became divided into churches, sects, and a growing band of mutually tolerant respectable religious bodies which certainly sought to bring in as many people as possible and yet which were clearly not 'churches' in the classic sense. It is these bodies which we normally call 'denominations'.

Denominations differ from sects in that they are not exclusive (that is, there is no real membership test of merit or grace) and they make relatively few demands of their members. People may choose to join but many members are born into the group. Like the church, the denomination has a professional ministry, it is large, and it is often associated with the comfortable classes. It thus represents a position intermediate between the sect and the church. However, it differs from both sect and church in one particularly important respect. Both the sect and the church think they have a monopoly of truth. Each says that it and it alone has the key to heaven. The denomination does not claim such exclusive access to the truth that saves. Rather it says that it has a particularly clear vision of the Christian message but allows that there are other religious bodies which also have much of the truth. The Congregationalists do not believe that Methodists are going to hell because they are not Congregationalists. Instead they concede that Methodists have as much right and can be partners in such common enterprises as foreign missions, evangelistic crusades, and social-welfare efforts.

The last two hundred years have seen the gradual evolution of churches and sects into denominations. The church form has been made untenable by the gradual increase in cultural pluralism and by the unwillingness of the state to continue to force reluctant people into the state church. The state churches of England, Scotland, Wales, and Ireland were slow to give up their privileges. Catholics in England and Wales were only allowed the vote in 1829. It was 1850 before the Catholic Church was allowed to restore its hierarchy in England and Wales, and anti-Catholic feeling in Scotland was so strong that it was a further twenty-eight years before the hierarchy was restored there. From 1847 Lionel de Rothschild was repeatedly elected to parliament for the City of London but could not take his seat because he refused to take a Christian oath. In 1858 a compromise allowed each House to revise its oath and Lionel's son Nathaniel became the first Jew to receive a peerage. Only in 1854, two hundred years after the first major wave of dissent from the Church of England, were non-Anglican students allowed to study at Oxford and Cambridge, and it was 1871 before religious tests for staff at those universities were abolished.

When all, or almost all, of the population belong to one religious organization, it is possible for those inside that organization to see their mission in terms of the church form and to behave like a church. Even the radical sectarians who depart from the church can continue to believe in it and hope that, either by winning the hearts of the people, or by a *coup d'état*, they will acquire the levers of power. But when a population becomes divided between a number of organizations, that fragmentation undermines the conditions for the church form in two ways. First, as the above examples illustrate, the struts of state support for a religious monopoly are kicked away and it becomes ever more difficult to imagine a state monopoly being reconstructed. Secondly, the dogmatists in both church and sect become influenced by the social psychology of the pluralistic culture. It is easy to believe that a religion is right in every detail when there is no alternative. Then it is not a matter of belief; it is simply an accurate reflection of how things are. To use the German phenomenologists' phrase, the 'taken-for-granted' worldview gains enormous strength from being constantly reinforced by such frequent communal occasions as rituals for birth, death, and marriage. The core beliefs are constantly reaffirmed through being daily uttered in public oaths and testimonies. In everyday interaction, members of the same community of faith unconsciously reaffirm their world-view by using such phrases as 'God willing'.

Every increase in competition challenges that taken-for-grantedness and makes certainty more difficult to maintain. If the competing faith belongs to some subordinate social minority, it can be dismissed as fitting only for that kind of people. Well-travelled Christians did not take the primitive religions they encountered seriously as plausible alternatives. Rather, they saw them as suitable for people of that state of intellectual development. But when small communities of socially similar people start to fragment so that some stay in the Church of Scotland and some go to the Free Church down the road and some attend a Baptist meeting around the corner, and you live and work with these people, it becomes more and more difficult to insist that your own link with God is unique and the others are all wrong. Gradually the way in which people hold their beliefs changes, so that the absolute certainty and the intolerance diminish and one ends up with the denominational position of supposing that all these organizations, in their different ways, are doing God's work.

If, in addition to this corrosive effect of cultural pluralism, the relaxation of state support is the main dynamic behind the evolution of the church into the denomination, the change in the sect has its roots in the decline of radicalism. In *The Social Sources of Denominationalism*, American theologian and historian H. R. Niebuhr noted that time and again what began life as a radical sect evolved into a comfortable denomination, on easy terms with the world. There are a number of reasons why this should have happened. The first generation of sectarians consciously sought the demands of the sect and made considerable sacrifices for their beliefs, which were then reflected in high levels of commitment. But each subsequent generation was born into the sect and, even when great effort is put into socializing the children into the sect's ideology, it is inevitable that what is given free will seem less valuable than that for which a high price has been paid.

The waning enthusiasm is further challenged by rising standards of living. By working diligently to glorify God and avoiding expensive and wasteful luxuries, the early generations of sectarians became prosperous. Their heirs thus had more to lose by remaining too much at odds with prevailing standards and patterns of consumption. They mixed with others of more elevated status than their parents and became embarrassed at the roughness and lack of sophistication of their place of worship, their uneducated ministers, and their folk hymns. They began to press for small changes which brought them ever closer to the established churches.

Although most sects begin as primitive democracies, with the equality of all believers and little or no formal organization, gradually a professional leadership cadre emerges. Especially after the death of the founding charismatic leaders, there is a need formally to structure the appointment, education, and training of the preachers and teachers who will sustain the movement. There will also be assets to manage: church buildings, schools, investment funds, and printing houses. With organization comes paid officials and such people have a vested interest in reducing the conflict between the sect and the surrounding society. They compare themselves to the clergy of other churches and want the same status and levels of education, training, and reward.

It is possible, usually by creating social barriers between themselves and the world, for sects to prevent the gradual relaxation of what makes them distinctive, but there are enough examples of sects evolving into denominations for us to suppose that the change is driven by some general principles of human behaviour. The changes in the Methodists in the three generations after the death of Wesley are a good example, as is the history of the British Quakers. The austere commitment of early followers, with their distinctive mode of plain dress (with wide-brimmed hats for the men who conspicuously refused to 'doff' them for the king) and distinctive forms of speech (for example, using 'thee' and 'thou' long after they had ceased to be common currency), gave way among those who came to be called 'Gay Quakers' to more conventional styles. The early Quakers would not have read a novel or attended the theatre, but the Gay Quakers (usually the offspring of increasingly wealthy merchants, manufacturers, and bankers) became more and more like the Church of England neighbours with whom they mixed as social equals. By the early nineteenth century, Barclays, Trittons, Gurneys, and Buxtons—the families whose businesses merged to form

Barclays Bank—were crossing over first into the evangelical wing of the Church of England, where several Barclays and Buxtons distinguished themselves as missionaries, and then disappearing into the mainstream.

As the sects compromise, so the cycle begins again. Not everyone has shared in the prosperity that has seen the sect rise. Some are still poor and dispossessed. They break away to find again a pristine and radical expression of Christianity. They found new sects. These in turn grow, produce further generations, create a professional clergy, and so on. In the English-speaking world one sees the phases laid down like sedimentary layers of rock: the first wave of dissent from Anglicanism gave us the Baptists, Congregationalists, and Quakers; the second wave gave us Methodism; the third, at the end of the nineteenth century, produced the Salvation Army and the Holiness Movement; and the fourth, at the start of this century, gave us Pentecostalism.

The national and international face of increased religious moderation was the ecumenical movement and its inter-church organizations. Not surprisingly, the need for interdenominational co-operation first impressed itself on those people promoting the Christian message in the least favourable circumstances: foreign missionaries and the activists of the Student Christian Movement (SCM) working in universities and colleges. First the evangelical Protestants began to co-operate. Then, in 1910, SCM leaders persuaded the 'high' or Catholic wing of the Church of England to attend an international missionary conference, and from those beginnings the ecumenical movement developed, bringing in first the Orthodox and Coptic churches and finally, in the 1960s, bringing on board the Roman Catholic Church, first with only observer status and then, in the 1980s, as a full member of various inter-church bodies which now encompass almost every shade of British Christianity.

To summarize thus far, the period from the Reformation to 1900 saw a fundamental change in the nature of Christian religion in Britain and its relation to the individual and the state. The rise of cultural pluralism and individualism undermined the church form of religion and saw sects flourish. The largest of these evolved into moderate and liberal denominations. The gradual relaxation of distinctiveness was accompanied by a series of reunions. In Scotland the majority of Presbyterians reunited in two stages (in 1900 and in 1927), leaving behind very small conservative and liberal rumps. The majority of the Methodist groups gradually united. Although England, Wales, and Scotland retained state churches, these came to view themselves (and be viewed by others) as denominations. The enormity of the changes can be readily perceived in the resonances of the term 'Nonconformist', which has gone from being a major (and in some places *the* major) mark of social identity to being a quaint and archaic reminder of the world destroyed by the First World War.

Changes in Funding Base

The changing status of the British state churches can be very clearly seen in the way they are funded. Although the details are slightly different in the four parts of the British Isles, the basic pattern was that, until the nineteenth century, the state churches were funded by the land they owned (religious officials either took the rental value or farmed it themselves) and by public taxation. Dissenters who wanted an alternative had to pay for it themselves and those of substance resented having to pay twice. They funded their clergy, church buildings, and church schools through the collection plate *and* paid taxes to a state church they did not accept. Through a number of reforms in the nineteenth century, this affront to individualist notions of fairness was addressed; the historic rights of the state churches were 'cashed up' and handed to those churches to manage themselves. Thus the funding of Britain's religious life was divided: the established churches had enormous capital reserves, the interest from which was used to subsidize a national parochial ministry (which could not be sustained solely from the voluntary contributions of attending members). The dissenting bodies relied exclusively on direct giving from members.

In this century the differences have gradually diminished. Rich dissenters left money to their organizations and thus created capital reserves which could subsidize present activity. At the same time the value of the historic assets of the state churches was eroded, partly by inflation and partly by poor investment decisions. Figures released in 1993 by the Church Commissioners, the body which handles the Church of England's resources, showed that continuing to invest in property after the boom of the early 1980s had taken almost a third off the assets, which had shrunk from £3 billion to £2.2 billion since 1989. In 1993 there was a £50 million shortfall between income and expenditure on clergy salaries and pensions.

It is ironic that the state churches managed to survive the growth of religious diversity without seriously having to rethink their mission only to have such reconsideration thrust on them by economic misfortune. Instead of offering their services evenly across the whole country, the Church of England and the Church of Scotland are now merging parishes and consolidating to become indistinguishable from the voluntary sects and denominations—organizations which are funded primarily by existing (or recently deceased) members to serve only their members.

Women and the Final Reformation of the Anglican Church

One of the key issues of the Reformation that then coloured the subsequent development and interaction of Protestants and Catholics was the character and status of the clergy. Most Protestant groups (radical sects such as the Brethren are the exception) accepted that having a group of full-time ministers who, by virtue of their piety, experience, training, and wisdom, were able to lead others was a good idea, but that the Protestant pastor was only one among equals. Though it dropped the insistence that its clergy be celibate, in retaining a spiritual hierarchy, the episcopal Church of England held on to a large part of the Roman Catholic idea that the priesthood was a distinct calling which should be marked off by a distinct way of life.

The Anglican clergy has changed under two sources of pressure. The gradual distancing from the state caused many church leaders (and many members of parliament) to feel that it was inappropriate for church matters to be dealt with by the elected legislature which now included very many non-Anglicans. At the same time the democratic structures of the Nonconformist denominations represented an attractively modern way of doing business. The result has been that the Church of England has gradually developed its own administrative, consultative, and legislative structures which allow considerable lay involvement and thus rather dent the notion of episcopal distinctiveness.

The development of modern societies has been characterized by an expansion of the population to whom 'rights' are allocated. In the matter of the right to vote, the small wealthy and powerful electorate was gradually augmented to encompass first men of little property, and then all men, and, finally, all adults. The expansion and 'normalization' of the clergy have followed a similar pattern. Women, who have long been a clear majority of members, attenders, and activists in European Christian churches, were long denied the right to do the special things that clergymen did. Precisely because they had no theological justification for regarding the clergy as spiritually distinctive, it was the radical Protestant sects which first gave leadership roles to women. The early Methodists allowed women preachers but then backtracked as the movement became more respectable. It is only in this century, after full political rights had been won by women, that the larger denominations ordained them. The liberal Scottish United Free Church ordained women in the 1930s and the Church of Scotland followed in the 1960s. In many denominations, it was the sister churches located in such former colonies as Australia, the United States, and Canada which first took the plunge. After decades of pressure from women within the church, in 1992 (reaffirmed a year later) the Church of England decided to ordain women to the priesthood. More than the doctrinal arguments that have periodically divided Anglican clergy, this move threatens the Church's unique position of straddling Protestant and Catholic traditions. Although it is too early to be clear about the scale of defections, it is possible that more than a hundred Anglican priests will defect to Rome. Already there have been high-profile conversions. Ann Widdicombe and John Selwyn Gummer, Anglicans who were prominent because they were also members of the Conservative Government, have joined the Roman Catholic Church.

The Decline of the Supernatural

The gradual shift in self-image from church and sect to denomination was accompanied by changes in key doctrines which can reasonably be summarized as a decline in the supernatural. In different organizations the changes came at different rates, but the general direction was the same. To get some idea of the extent of change, we can consider the text of the Apostles' Creed, which, with slightly differing emphases, summarizes the common ground of Christianity.

THE APOSTLES' CREED

I believe in God the Father Almighty, Maker of heaven and earth. And in Jesus Christ His only Son our Lord, who was conceived by the Holy Ghost, Born of the Virgin Mary, Suffered under Pontious Pilate, Was Crucified, dead and buried; He descended into hell; The third day He rose again from the dead; He ascended into heaven, and sitteth on the right hand of God the Father Almighty; From thence he shall come to judge the quick and the dead.

I believe in the Holy Ghost; the holy catholic (or universal) Church; the Communion of Saints; the Forgiveness of sins; the Resurrection of the body; and the Life everlasting.

We can never be sure what went on in the minds of people of other times and cultures, but we can be pretty confident that, until the middle of the last century, almost everyone who recited the Creed took it at something like face value; if they meant something else, they would have said something else! They believed in an actual God who really did make heaven and earth in pretty much the way described in the Old Testament book of Genesis. They believed that Christ was the Son of God, was the product of a miraculous virgin birth, was killed, and went to the real place of hell, before being bodily resurrected and then ascending into the real place of heaven. Furthermore, they believed that the Bible differed from other books in being the word of God, and, though they could recognize metaphor when they saw it (no one ever thought that Jesus was a sheep just because he is described as the Lamb of God), they did not think that the Bible miracles were metaphors. Lot's wife was turned into a pillar of salt. Jonah was swallowed by a big fish.

Gradually over the last hundred years mainstream Christianity has moved to a quite different interpretation of these things. God is rarely thought of as an actual person but as some sort of vague power or our own consciences. The Bible is no longer the word of God but a historical book with some useful ethical and moral guidelines for living. Miracles either did not really happen or they were natural phenomena misunderstood by ignorant peasants. Christ is no longer the Son of God but an exemplary prophet and teacher. The costs and rewards of religion were internalized. Heaven and hell ceased to be real places and became psychological states. Hell, in so far as the term was used at all, was no longer a venue for future and indefinite actual suffering but the mental state of alienation, anomie, incompleteness, or just unhappiness. Likewise heaven, which remained in the currency for a little longer, became happiness, completeness, personal fulfilment, and the like.

These changes had two obvious values in adjusting Christianity to the modern world. First, they saved most of the specific content of the faith from refutation by increasingly popular secular knowledge. However, as I shall argue in Chapter Five, the clash of ideas between religion and science was not the main reason for changes in the former. There is ample evidence that we can believe things long after the best evidence points elsewhere. Where a sub-society of like-minded people can be gathered, it is always possible to maintain a deviant subculture of beliefs. Much more important in understanding why one set of ideas replaces another are the social relationships between groups and the general social climate in which beliefs have to be sustained. More detrimental than the external cognitive threat from scientific knowledge was the internal fragmentation of the religious culture. By being reworked to turn them from factual and historical claims about the world to propositions about internal psychological states, religious claims ceased to be matters of bitter social conflict. If heaven and hell are psychological states, there is less necessity to argue about their nature and how to avoid them.

Harry Fosdick Emerson, a leading liberal Protestant clergyman of the 1930s, said that the starting-point of Christianity was faith in human personality. The problem of increasing irreligion was not that people were going to go to hell but that 'multitudes of people are living not bad but frittered lives—split, scattered, uncoordinated'.[3] The solution was a religion which would 'furnish an inward spiritual dynamic for radiant and triumphant living'. Religion as a relationship to the supernatural was replaced by religion as personal therapy. It was no longer about glorifying God but about personal growth. To put the point in traditional sociological language, shared religion, in addition to the primary purpose or manifest function of linking this world with the divine, has always had latent functions or secondary consequences. Previously, those latent functions have been primarily social and have been directed to the lives of societies and communities, to the preservation of shared moral values and social mores, to an identity beyond the individual. Now the secondary benefits of religion are individualized and they have largely displaced the primary purpose. Primitive people intended to worship God and accidentally maintained the cohesion of their society. We pursue personal satisfaction and accidentally worship God.

Along with the disappearance of much of the supernaturalism which used to lie at the heart of Christianity, the other great change has been in the implicit images of the *self*. Are we basically good and made bad by our circumstances or are we essentially bad and made good only by socialization and social control? The traditional Christian view is that, since the Fall and the expulsion from the Garden of Eden, we have been bad and that only the dramatic intervention of God and the subordination of the self to the will of God can make us good again. Liberal Protestantism rejected that and supposed, as one sees in Norman Vincent Peale's *Power of Positive Thinking* (first published in the 1950s and still being reprinted), that the self is improvable and even perfectible. In the 1950s and 1960s there was a clear division between liberal and conservative Christians, with evangelical, fundamentalist, and pentecostal Protestants defining themselves against this trend, but the next twenty years saw even these groups being influenced by the secularization of their religion. Though some of the traditional language remains—evangelicals still insist that the historical claims of their religion are factually correct and that we all need to be again'—much of the content has gone. Suffering, for example, is rarely presented as part of God's inscrutable plan, to be humbly accepted. Self-denial is *passé*. Even radical Protestant sectarians enjoy the products of affluence that were once dismissed as the work of the devil. In the 1960s an elderly Presbyterian told me the following joke: 'Why don't Baptists make love standing up? God might see and think they are dancing!' Now only the most radical wing of the Brethren movement would denounce dancing. Dining out, watching television, going to the movies, dressing well, and wearing make-up are unremarkable in conservative Protestant circles. Most importantly, the basic shift in thinking about the self has now permeated evangelical circles as religion there has also taken on the mantle of personal therapy. The following are titles of best-selling evangelical books in the United States in the 1980s: *The Undivided Self: Bringing your Whole Life in Line with God's Will, You can Become the Person You Want to Be, The Healthy Personality and the Christian Life, How to Become your Own Best Self,* and *Self-Esteem: The New Reformation.* God is still there, but he is no longer the strict father whose job it is to smash the human self and bring us to see our own worthlessness. He is the psychotherapist who can help us to be more fulfilled and to achieve more in this life.

Finally, the ecumenism of mainstream Christianity has now penetrated evangelicalism. When American evangelist Billy Graham first began his missions to Britain in the 1950s, he was sponsored in the main only by evangelical ministers, and those who 'came forward' at his rallies were referred only to Protestant churches. Now he accepts invitations from liberal Protestant and Catholic churches and in arranging for the further counselling of converts accepts a sweeping definition of 'Christian' churches. This is not to say that evangelical Protestants and Roman Catholics have entirely given up claims to a distinctively superior religion, but they have mostly abandoned the church/sect claim to a unique possession of the truth.

The Cult

If the above gives us an idea of what we mean by 'church', 'sect', and 'denomination', we can now briefly consider the fourth major form of religious organization. Ernst Troeltsch identified a distinct element of the Christian tradition which he called 'mysticism'. Unlike the other forms, this was a highly individualistic expression, varying with personal experiences and interpretations. The organized form that corre-

---

THE HARD CHOICE OF PLURALISM

The choice faced by churches in a culturally plural society can be clearly seen in the following two recent events. In 1991 one-fifth of the clergy of England and Wales signed a petition opposing any coming-together in worship of peoples of different faiths. The petitioners asserted that 'Salvation is offered *only* through Jesus Christ', who is 'the only Saviour' and 'the only way to God'. On the other side of the argument stand the clergy associated with the 'Sea of Faith' movement, which takes a thoroughly relativist and inclusivist view of religious revelation. In 1993 the Revd Anthony Freeman became the first priest this century to be dismissed for religious dissent. He was removed from his clergy training post after publishing *God in Us: A Case for Christian Humanism*, which argued against the traditional Christian conception of God as a supernatural being, and was given a year in which to consider his position. In 1994, when he did not recant, he was removed from his parish.

---

sponds to Troeltsch's idea is the *cult*: a loosely knit group organized around some common themes and interests but lacking any sharply defined and exclusive belief system. Each individual member is the final authority as to what constitutes the truth or the path to salvation. The cult, like the denomination, is tolerant and understanding of its own members (indeed it is so tolerant that it hardly has 'members'; instead it has consumers who pick and choose those bits of its product that suit them). In movements such as spiritualism, New Thought, and much of the flying-saucer movement, so vague and broad are the range of accepted teachings that the notion of 'heresy' is meaningless. Typically, such organized groups as one finds within cultic movements are short lived. People drift in and out of them. Where adherents usually leave sects because they come to disagree with some key belief, those who depart from cult groups after any significant period of involvement usually leave because they have got what they want from the new knowledge or therapy and feel free to move on to some other revelation. Astrological groups, for example, tend to lose members once they have learnt the rudiments of astrological-chart construction.

Refining the Distinctions

The distinctions between churches, sects, denominations, and cults can now be summarized in a very simple model. Almost all the

differences in such crucial characteristics as membership requirements, structure, and relations with other religious organizations can
be understood if we ask just two questions about a religion: how does it
view its own revelation in comparison with other religious organizations and how is it regarded by the wider society. These two principles
yield four categories which identify the major divisions discussed.

Figure 1.1 A Typology of Ideological Organizations

		External conception	
		Respectable	Deviant
Internal conception	Uniquely legitimate	CHURCH	SECT
	Pluralistically legitimate	DENOMINATION	CULT

Source: Roy Wallis, *The Road to Total Freedom: A Sociological Analysis of Scientology*
(London: Heinemann, 1976), 13.

Most Mormons believe that their organization offers the only way to
God. Hence they try to persuade people to join the Mormons. For
Mormons, the Church of Jesus Christ of Latter-day Saints—to give it its
proper name—is *uniquely legitimate.* The Roman Catholic Church has
traditionally taken the same view, although in some settings it is now
moderating its claims. The Exclusive Brethren also take the view that
they and they alone have the Way. But there is considerable difference
in the popularity, acceptability, and prestige of the Catholic Church, the
Mormons, and the Exclusive Brethren. Consider the way the media
treat them. It is common to see documentaries which are highly critical
of the tight way in which the Brethren socialize their children to
become the next generation of the Brethren. It is rare to see similar
arguments being put about Catholic schooling or about the Church's
insistence that the children of mixed marriages be raised as Catholics.
Hence we would say that the Catholics are a 'church' but the Brethren
are a 'sect'. The position of the Mormons is interesting and allows us to
appreciate the *relative* nature of these terms. The Mormons began as a
highly deviant (and much persecuted) sect. In many parts of the world,
they remain a deviant sect. But in Utah they have achieved such numerical superiority as to be able to act as if they formed a 'church'.

Consider the bottom half of Figure 1.1. What the denomination—the Methodists, now, would be an example—and the cult have in common is that they do not claim a unique possession of the truth. They think they have something to offer, that you might be better off being a Methodist than a Baptist, but they recognize other organizations as being every bit as valid as themselves. Again what separates them is the top line: the extent to which they have succeeded in establishing themselves. The Methodists are a respectable part of our social and cultural landscape; cults are not.

The difference in self-image between the church and sect, on the one hand, and the denomination and cult, on the other, produces a considerable difference in vulnerability. Because they are so demanding and make such exclusive claims for their own product, churches and sects tend to be brittle. Their strength is of the sort that can, when subjected to the right sort of pressure, lead to large cracks and splintering. The denomination and the cult are vulnerable in a very different way. Denominations and cults are relatively weak institutions in that their beliefs and practices are barely distinguishable from those of a large number of similar groups. Though inertia keeps most people where they were raised, it is ideologically easy to move from the Church of England (now a denomination despite its title) to the Methodists to the Baptists and back again. It is almost as easy to shift right out of organized religion. The tolerance of the denomination removes most reasons for trying to recruit new members by conversion. Indeed, many Christians no longer accept the validity of conversion; in 1994 George Carey, the Archbishop of Canterbury, withdrew his patronage from an organization dedicated to converting Jews to Christianity. And apart from a sentimental desire to see one's children follow in one's footsteps, there is no powerful reason to work hard to socialize one's children into the doctrines of one's denomination. Cults are similarly unable to press the need for orthodoxy on their followers or extract any great commitment from them. Those who are interested are selective in their acceptance of the doctrines and practices. They pick this or that bit and synthesize it with what they have acquired from other cults. For the types of religion on the top line of the model, the danger is factionalism and schism; for those on the bottom line, it is low levels of commitment and drifting.

Religion and Ethnic Conflict

Historians and social scientists have long been aware of the role of religion as social cement; shared rituals and shared beliefs bind people together, and the divinity that they invoke justifies the mundane culture. Emile Durkheim went so far as to present the social solidarity functions as the *cause* of religion. What is not so often noted is the logical accompaniment to the idea that a commonly worshipped God holds a people together: religion often divides one group from another. The tribal or national God justifies the actions of his people against the heathen by providing the ultimate justification for dividing the world into 'them' and 'us'. We are doing God's will; they deserve everything they get.

Since the Reformation, Great Britain has been largely free of ethnic conflict informed by religion. At times the English, Scots, and Welsh have drawn on their religious differences to accentuate their political divisions, but the potential for religious differences to foment social conflict has been limited by the fact that each region has operated a variant of a common tradition. The nearest equivalent to the warring between Christian, Muslim, and Druze in Lebanon or Muslim, Catholic Christian, and Orthodox Christian in Yugoslavia is the battle with Roman Catholicism, which gives the Irish conflict part of its intractable character and accounts for most of the sectarian conflict seen in Britain and Northern Ireland.

The distinctiveness of Ireland has its origins in the failure of the Reformation, either as a popular movement or as a political programme imposed by the élite. Protestantism had little direct impact on the Irish church and came largely from two external sources. Under James VI's policy of granting lands confiscated from rebellious Irish lords to British settlers, from 1607 over 10,000 Scottish Presbyterians were attracted to Ireland, most of them settling in the north-eastern province of Ulster. The Episcopalians were largely English settlers, and their legally established 'Church of Ireland' was a grandly misnamed imposition. To appreciate why those divisions have remained salient for over 400 years, it is important to remember that Catholicism and Protestantism were not just two religions that happened not to be the same. Protestantism was a conscious departure from the medieval church, and what remained consciously reconstructed itself in opposition to the doctrines and practices of the Reformers. Protestantism and Catholicism evolved in opposition to each other. Remember also that Protestants settled in Ireland at a time when people took religion seriously. That the various populations coming into economic and political conflict identified themselves by opposing religions discouraged (though it did not prevent) intermarriage and allowed them to develop invidious stereotypes in which each claimed social and civic virtues which the other supposedly lacked and then explained these virtues by the possession of the correct faith. In so far as Protestant farmers recognized that they were more prosperous, they saw this as a result of them being diligent, hard-working, God-fearing, and so on, and not as a result of government policy giving them the better lands.

There were times when the three sides of the triangle—Scots Presbyterian, English Episcopalian, and Irish Catholic—could have formed other alliances. Inspired by the French Revolution, a number of liberal Ulster Presbyterians joined Irish nationalists in the United Irishmen revolt. But as the Catholic Irish became more powerful, the two Protestant groups drew closer together. In the 1830s, when there were moves to remove the legally established and privileged position of the Episcopalian Church of Ireland, leading Presbyterian clerics sided with the Episcopalians on the grounds that having an established Protestant church, even the wrong one, was better than a free market in religion which Roman Catholics would dominate because of their greater numbers. That argument was lost. As it did in the other countries of the United Kingdom, the British government put maintaining social order above defending the faith and disestablished the Church of Ireland. Although Irish nationalists made a great fuss of the one or two leading Protestants in their various movements, the political polarization became complete by the end of the nineteenth century. By the time the eventually successful Irish Home Rule movement was destroying British politics, the Ireland for which nationalists sought independence would clearly be an Irish and Catholic Ireland. The vast majority of Protestants sided with the Union cause and attempted to remain British.

The partition of Ireland in 1921 created an overwhelmingly Catholic Irish Free State and allowed the north-eastern six counties of Ulster, dominated by Protestant Unionists but with a sizeable Catholic minority, to remain part of the United Kingdom. The Free State was Catholic by virtue of numbers, but, when he became Prime Minister in 1932, Éamon de Valera went further in assigning to the Catholic Church a privileged position in the constitution he wrote for the Irish Republic.

Although the conflict in Ireland, now reduced to the Ulster Troubles, is not *about* religion, it is none the less heavily informed by religion in that the religion of each side is an important part of its ethnic identity. Although the leaders of the main churches have consistently denied legitimation to those groups in Ulster which pursue their political goals by terror, the churches have remained firmly associated with the

23

competing political positions, clergymen are active in promoting the interests of their ethnic group, and religion remains a thoroughly successful predictor of voting and of constitutional preferences.

There were echoes of the Irish conflict in those parts of Britain most affected by Irish migration. Apart from small pockets of Catholicism in the highlands and the north-east, Scotland after the Reformation was a thoroughly Protestant country. A census in 1780 claimed only 6,600 Catholics below the Highland line. Another source says there were only 50 Catholics in the city of Glasgow in 1795, but by 1829 there were 25,000 and by 1843 twice that number. Edinburgh in 1829 had about 14,000 Catholics where thirty years earlier there had been fewer than 1,000. By 1840 10 per cent of the Scottish population were either Irish migrants or their descendants and they were heavily concentrated in Glasgow and the west central lowlands, Edinburgh, and Dundee.

Seasonal migration from Ireland to Scotland had been common for centuries, but the combination of industrialization in Scotland creating work in the towns and cities (and in the fields to replace the rural Scots who were attracted to the towns) and a series of famines in Ireland turned seasonal migration into permanent settlement. That the arrival of the Irish coincided with the arrival of all the social problems of industrialization—slum housing, crime and vice, the erosion of employers' responsibility for their workers, alcoholism—meant that many Scots were ready to blame the Irish for those problems. What further fuelled the fires of conflict was the fact that only three-quarters of the Irish migrants were Catholics. The rest were Ulster Protestants, people who already had a long history of ethnic conflict with Irish Catholics and who brought with them their fraternal organization.

The Orange Order was so-named after Prince William of Orange, who was invited by the English parliament to take the British throne in place of the Catholic James, duke of York. James retreated to Ireland and there mobilized an Irish Catholic army which laid siege to the city of Londonderry but was finally beaten after battles at the Boyne, Enniskillen, and Aughrim. As the slogans still painted on Belfast gable walls remind us, that was in 1690.

The Ulster Protestant tradition very readily fitted with the Protestant culture of lowland Scotland and was quickly adopted by groups of skilled Scottish workers who saw their culture challenged by Roman Catholicism and their hard-won industrial power threatened by impoverished Irish people willing to work for less and to be hired as strike-breakers. Irrespective of how little any one of them actually possessed such virtues, the native Scots saw themselves as literate, educated, diligent, temperant, democratic, and hard-working. With a degree of truth, they saw the Irish as illiterate, ill-educated, slothful, undisciplined, and in thrall to their priests.

The religious, social, economic, and political differences gelled into often bitter social conflict that periodically erupted into open violence when moves such as the removal of anti-Catholic discriminatory laws brought the issue to the fore. There were anti-Catholic riots in Glasgow and Edinburgh. Catholic chapels were burnt down. Shops owned by Catholics were looted. A generalized prejudice against the Irish became widespread and deeply embedded, as we can see from the following snippets of court reporting from the Glasgow-based *North British Daily Mail*: 'Yesterday at the Central Police Court, an ape-faced, small-headed Irishman . . .', 'An impudent Irish ruffian . . .', 'Pat O'Shannon, a startled looking Irish tailor . . .', 'Two surly-looking sons of the Emerald Isle . . .'.

Like migrant minorities the world over, the Irish and their descendants responded to their hostile reception by turning inwards and forming a ghetto in which almost all community life was organized around and by the Catholic Church. Glasgow Celtic Football Club was formed by Catholic priests as an outlet for recreation and as a way of raising funds for the poor of the East End of Glasgow. The constitution of the first Hibernian Football Club in Edinburgh required that members be *practising* Catholics. The interests of the Catholic Church and the interests of the immigrants interacted to reinforce each other. For the migrants the Church was their major social institution, the one thing they had in common and the only source of communal leadership, so they turned to it. At the same time, the Church was concerned about losing its members and discouraged assimilation.

Crucial to the structure of the ghetto was the Catholic Church's insistence on preserving its own schools. Until the second half of the nineteenth century most schooling was provided by the churches, which worked well so long as there was a single national church with an even geographical spread, but the fragmentation of Scottish Presbyterianism into competing alternatives and the inability of the largest of them to shift resources to deal with the massive flow of people from the country to the city made it clear to political leaders that the state would have to become responsible for schooling. Under an 1872 act, the Presbyterian churches handed their schools to the state, to be managed by local school boards. However, the Catholic Church feared that its offspring would become converted to Protestantism and refused to join. As with the English Nonconformists and their resentment at paying church rates, the Catholics were left in the position that those well enough off to be liable for tax were funding a state system which they did not use while also financing their own confessional schools. Despite heroic efforts in fund-raising, Catholic schools remained second rate. Eventually an acceptable accommodation was arrived at with the 1918 Education Act. The state would almost entirely fund Catholic schools, but the Church would remain in full control. Most importantly, the Church would select staff.

Although the above details concern the Irish in Scotland, an almost identical story could be told for those who settled in Liverpool, Manchester, the north-east of England, and London. What is significant is the speed with which the Irish ghetto broke down after the 1920s when the temporary solution to the Irish problem of partitioning the island removed Irish politics from the British agenda for fifty years. First within their own ghettos and then broadening out from them, the descendants of the Irish prospered. The gradual secularization of British life made religion less and less of an issue. Of particular importance in assimilation was the involvement of the Irish in the British labour movement. In other European countries, Catholics formed their own 'Christian Democratic' parties and trade unions. In 1930s Britain, once the more militantly socialist organizations had been replaced by the more moderate British Labour Party, Catholic bishops dropped their opposition to labour politics and many Catholics became involved alongside Protestant workers, which prevented them becoming an easy political target. For a short time, there was polarization in Glasgow and Liverpool, with the skilled Protestant working class in the Orange Lodges and Freemasons supporting the 'Conservative and Unionist' Party (so-called because it was in favour of maintaining the Union of Great Britain and Ireland) and the Catholic working class supporting Labour candidates, but Protestant workers soon came to put their class interests before their religio-ethnic identity and voted Labour. With sectarianism an issue in only a few parts of the United Kingdom and for those people least likely to vote Conservative, the Conservative Party dropped its interest in Orangeism and the word 'Unionist' was allowed to slip from its name.

In his detailed studies of English Catholicism, Hornsby-Smith has shown the strong connection between the upward mobility of Catholics from the 1930s and the gradual break-up of a strong Catholic community. In the late 1930s, over 70 per cent of Catholics who married did so within the community. By the late 1970s, this was just over 30 per cent. The number of Catholics who said that half or more of their friends were Catholics fell over the same period from almost 60 to under 40 per cent. At the same time, commitment to the Church declined, with church-attendance patterns moving to the British norm (which will be discussed in detail in the next chapter) and the Church relaxing its expectations of the laity as it became more like a Protestant denomination.

As we now know only too well, the partition of Ireland may have removed the Irish question from British politics, but it did not end the conflict between the two ethnic groups, which erupted again in 1969 as Catholics in Northern Ireland first protested against their subordinate position in Ulster and then followed their success into destabilizing the old Stormont regime by pressing for the removal of Northern Ireland from the United Kingdom. As we will see in the next chapter, the continued political conflict has kept religious identification and involvement, on both sides of the Ulster divide, extremely high, while other European countries have become increasingly secular.

Conclusion

The changes in the nature and position of religion over almost five centuries cannot easily be compressed into a short chapter, and whole areas (Wales, for example) and periods have been omitted in this review, but I hope enough detail has been given to provide an overall sense of the major changes in British Christianity and a brief guide to the central beliefs of those people and organizations that have done most to shape that history. In the briefest possible summary, I want to suggest that the *church* form of religion was made untenable by the cultural pluralism, egalitarianism, and individualism that came with economic modernization. The major trend in Britain was the gradual evolution of *church* and *sect* towards the form of religion we have called 'denominational'.

Further Reading

There are a large number of excellent histories of British religion. The rich literature of church histories which focus on the internal workings of religious institutions and their relations with the state has been complemented by excellent studies of the changing nature of popular involvement in the churches. Fine examples are Callum Brown, *A Social History of Religion in Scotland since 1730* (London: Methuen, 1987), and Alan D. Gilbert, *Religion and Society in Industrial England: Church, Chapel and Social Change 1740–1914* (London: Longmans, 1976). An excellent work which looks at religion in the European context is Hugh McLeod, *Religion and the People of Western Europe 1789–1970* (Oxford: Oxford University Press, 1981). The best available single source is Sheridan Gilley and W. J. Sheils (eds.), *A History of Religion in Britain: Practice and Belief from Pre-Roman Times to the Present* (Oxford: Blackwell, 1994), which contains twenty-six erudite but very readable essays.

On the place of religion in the Irish conflict, see John Fulton, *The Tragedy of Belief* (Oxford: Clarendon Press, 1991), and Steve Bruce, *God Save Ulster: The Religion and Politics of Paisleyism* (Oxford: Oxford University Press, 1986). On the Catholic community in Britain, see Tom Gallagher, *Glasgow: The Uneasy Peace* (Manchester: Manchester University Press, 1987), and Michael P. Hornsby-Smith, *The Changing Parish: A Study of Parishes, Priests and Parishioners after Vatican II* (London: Routledge, 1989).

Chapter Two

The Present

As we age, it is increasingly easy to fall into the trap of thinking that our lives and hence our times are uniquely interesting. It is common now to talk of our age as 'post-modern', as though it were radically different from the world of our parents or grandparents. Usually what is meant by that designation is that we are uniquely self-regarding and ironic. Compared to our naïve forebears, we no longer simply act in this or that way, but consciously and often cynically experiment with 'life-styles'. It is supposed that the massive increase in the speed and range of telecommunications has destroyed the integrity of particular local or national cultures and made us all sovereign consumers in a global supermarket of options. This post-modernist vision is, of course, an exaggeration—an unwarranted extension from the culture and society of the metropolitan centre to the country at large. Highgate and Islington are not the United Kingdom, though their denizens often act and speak as though they were.

None the less, Britain has changed enormously in the half-century since my father returned to it after the Second World War. Consider the nature of work. There has been a major shift from the manufacture of industrial goods to the manufacture of consumer goods and then to the provisions of services. Fewer people now have full-time secure jobs in large companies which they could expect to serve all their working lives; part-time and precarious (if sometimes well-paid) employment in short-lived enterprises is becoming the norm. With the dismantling and privatization of once-nationalized industries and of the Civil Service, public service is disappearing, both as a career and as an ethic. Divorce is commonplace, as is the raising of children in unconventional (usually single-mother) households. More than a quarter of live births are outside marriage. Forty per cent of women with children under 5 work, 10 per cent of them full-time. The invention of the oral contraceptive radically changed attitudes to sex. Homosexuality came out of the closet and got its own programmes on television. Though the

1980s has seen a widening of the gulf between rich and poor, most of us now enjoy a prosperity that was unimaginable in the Britain of the 1950s (when there was still rationing). One reflection of that is longer life. From 1938 to 1990, life expectancy for the average man increased from 60 to 72, and for the average woman from 65 to 78. Over the same period the proportion of people over 64 rose from 9 to 16 per cent.

With wealth has come increased leisure. In 1900 the average British manual worker worked a fifty-hour week. The typical working week is now only 80 per cent of that figure. Holidays are longer and more frequent. For many Britons cheap foreign travel is only an opportunity to do what they do at home but with fewer clothes on. None the less, the average Briton now travels farther and more often than ever before and the enormous diversity of cultural experiences found abroad is repeated at home with the mushrooming of ethnic food outlets and the appearance of once-exotic food and drink on the shelves of supermarkets in Aberdeen, Aberystwyth, and Abingdon.

The post-war period has also seen the invention of youth. Rising standards of living and the expansion of higher education (63,000 university students in 1938; 383,000 in 1989) have created a charmed space in which young people are given opportunities to act as autonomous individuals as yet unconstrained by the responsibilities that go with work, a family, and a mortgage.

All of this is said by way of background to considering the present nature and state of religion in Britain. In the context of this upheaval, how could religion have remained unchanged? In the briefest of summaries, I would describe the major trends of the religious life of the British in the post-war period as a decline in popular involvement in the main Christian churches, a corresponding and related decline in the popularity of religious beliefs outside the churches, a small shift to the 'right' in Protestantism, an increase in the popularity of non-Christian religions (explained largely by the arrival of significant bodies of immigrants), and a small but very interesting increase in the popularity and respectability of what were once deviant supernatural beliefs and practices. Ethnic-minority religion will be examined in Chapter Three and the New Age is discussed in Chapter Four. Here I want to look closely at what is known about Christian belief and practice.

Given the frequency with which 'decline' and its synonyms will be used in this chapter, we might begin by reminding ourselves that God and his worship remain an important part of the lives of very many people. To put it in some sort of context, in 1992 there were still close to 50,000 churches in the United Kingdom, which is one for every 940 adults and two churches for every one Post Office and for every three public houses.

Institutional Religion

Church, State, and Clergy

Whatever they have gained in the separation of church and state, the major Christian denominations have lost a great deal of power and influence. Current books on class and power do not even bother to mention the clergy. The state churches used to be powerful precisely because they were branches of the state. When they ceased to be arms of government, they remained influential because they recruited their senior clergy from the same class, the same schools and universities, and even the same families as did the government. The main Nonconformist churches had considerable political clout in the second half of the nineteenth century because the then-powerful Liberal Party represented their interests.

The gradual distancing of the state churches from the state and the freeing of the Nonconformists from close ties with parties which might form the government have allowed the British churches to rediscover the prophetic role of religion, challenging the government to righteousness, but that freedom has been bought at the price of the government listening to them. Frequently during the Conservative governments led by Margaret Thatcher (1979–90), the Church of England disappointed the Prime Minister. Its 1982 report *The Church and the Bomb* was profoundly critical of Britain's nuclear policy and the 1985 report *Faith in the City* attacked Thatcher's economic liberalism. When asked to stage a service to mark victory over Argentina in the Falklands War, the Archbishop of Canterbury and the Dean of St Paul's Cathedral very publicly distanced themselves from the government by making sure that the tone was one of thanksgiving rather than triumphalism. In so completely changing, from establishment to opposition, the Church of England has especially aroused the ire of Conservatives, but it is not alone in its critical role. The distinctive history of the Roman Catholic Church in England (and its subordination to the Vatican) makes it reluctant to engage in public rows, but the Methodist Conference has regularly voiced its opposition to Tory party policies, as has the Church of Scotland. Since the creation of the United Kingdom parliament, the Church of Scotland has had something of an additional role as the only elected representative national body in Scotland and this has been amplified by the growing perception that the British government does not speak for Scots. Since the 1950s the voting patterns of England and

Scotland have been steadily diverging. The Thatcher governments were elected by English voters. Thatcher's third election victory in 1987 saw Scotland vote overwhelmingly for the Labour Party; of seventy-two parliamentary seats in Scotland, only ten were won by Conservatives.

The reasons why the churches have been so critical of government policy can be briefly summarized. Thatcherism aimed to combine the liberal economics of the free market (which could be read by critics as allowing the weakest members of society to go to the wall) with reactionary social and moral policy. With some notion of Christian responsibility to the weak and a preference for charity, tolerance, and understanding over rectitude, the churches have found themselves defending an old-fashioned paternalistic conservativism in economic matters and promoting quite liberal socio-moral positions.

Leading Conservatives respond to such criticism from bodies that they expect to promote 'traditional values' by asserting that the senior church officials are out of touch with their members. In one sense this is the case: the major denominations can no longer command the obedience even of their committed members. Brave and radical initiatives such as the Church of England's *Faith in the City* programme mobilize little but fine words. Even on matters which are seen as being part of religion's now narrower remit (such as sexual or socio-moral issues), the churches cannot command with any hope of being followed. Even the Catholic Church, long seen by Protestant critics as having undue power over its constituency, is unable to control the actions of its people, as can be seen very clearly on the question of artificial birth control. The Church issued an authoritative ruling very much at odds with prevailing modern sentiment. The vast majority of its members choose to go with the prevailing secular sentiment.

This century has seen a marked change in the size and social composition of the clergy. The novels of Jane Austen in the eighteenth century and Anthony Trollope in the nineteenth show the church as a profession thought suitable for the younger sons of the gentry and for poor but clever men on the make. With the right patron to promote his interest and see him appointed to richly endowed 'livings', an ambitious man could view the clergy as an occupation desirable by the prevailing secular standards. In 1860 all the Church of England bishops had some connection with the peerage and the landed gentry. By 1960 no more than twenty-three of forty-three had such links. Now there are none, and poor but ambitious men become accountants, stockbrokers, and lawyers.

In 1900 there were just over 20,000 Church of England clerics. By 1984 that had halved to just over 10,000. As always we need to think of these numbers relative to the growth of the population as a whole, which went from around 32.5 million to over 50 million in the same period. In the largest of the dissenting bodies—the Methodists—there was some growth from 1900 to 1950—from 3,800 to 4,700 ministers—and then a rapid decline so that in 1993 there were only some 2,500.

In comparing the fortunes of the clergy one has to recall that churches, sects, and denominations have very different structures. In the nineteenth century the Catholic Church managed to service a very large population with very few professionals because it repeated its rituals in very large buildings where a small number of priests could cater for large numbers of laity. It could also run a very cost-effective operation in that, without wives and children to support, its celibate priests could be sustained on very low salaries. From 1900 to 1970 there was steady growth in the number of Catholic priests in England and Wales (from 2,300 in 1900 to 6,200 in 1970), many of them recruited from Eire and Northern Ireland, but this has since turned into decline, which has been exacerbated by the way that the Church has changed to become more democratic and participatory. Catholics now expect not the distant authority figure but the listening, chummy counsellor and therapist who involves his laity as equals, and that model of the church requires more not fewer priests. As the descendants of the Irish have become thoroughly assimilated, so their distinctly high levels of popular involvement have fallen, and this has been reflected in the decline in the numbers of men coming forward for ordination. The total number of priests is now around 6,000 and new ordinations are well below replacement levels.

At the start of the century there were about 3,600 ministers in the various Presbyterian churches in Scotland: 1,828 in the state Church of Scotland, 1,144 in the Free Church, and 631 in the United Presbyterian Church. As the various strands of Presbyterianism united, so the total fell markedly, as the wasteful duplication of the previous decades of competition was taken out of the system. In 1950 there were 2,751 in the Church of Scotland, 117 in the two remnants of the Free Church, and 85 continuing in the United Free Church; a total of 2,953. The contraction has since continued. In 1990 there were only 1,250 ministers in the Church of Scotland and less than 200 in the other Presbyterian churches. We thus see the same general picture as with the Church of England: the total number of religious professionals has been cut by more than half in a period when the total population has increased; in this case, from 4.5 million to over 5 million.

As we see in Table 2.1, the age profile of the clergy of the Church of England has changed markedly this century. First, and abruptly, the

Table 2.1 Church of England Clergy and Male Teachers, by Age, 1901–1988 (%)

Age	Church of England clergy						Male teachers
	1901	1921	1951	1961	1977	1988	1961
Under 40	33	20	21	22	34	12	52
40–9	23	22	20	25	23	28	28
50–9	19	24	18	30	24	39	18
60–4	8	12	10	9	10	17	4
65 and over	18	22	30	14	11	4	0

Note: Figures are rounded, so percentages may not total 100.

Sources: Leslie Paul, The Deployment and Payment of the Clergy (London, Church Information Office, 1966); Douglas Davies, Charles Watkins, and Michael Winter, Church and Religion in Rural England (Edinburgh: T. and T. Clark, 1991); Stewart Ranson, Alan Bryman, and Bob Hinings, Clergy, Ministers and Priests (London: Routledge and Kegan Paul, 1977).

First World War removed a generation of young ordinands, and the Second World War discouraged their replacement; but, as we see in comparing clerics with male teachers in 1961, peacetime did not see young men returning to the ministry. The introduction of old age pensions and the acceptance of the principle of retirement took out the very elderly clergy in the late 1950s, but the most recent figures—1988—show that the age profile remains skewed. We can understand this if we note that motives for ordination have changed. The church is now a haven for people driven largely by 'other-worldly' concerns. As the conventional attractions of the job have declined, so personal piety has become more important and an increasing proportion of ordinands are people who opt for the church after becoming disillusioned with a secular career. Recruits to the church may be respected for their selflessness. Indeed, they may be more respected now that the cynical response of many working-class people that religion is 'a good racket if you can get in on it'[1] has been undermined by the breaking of the close ties between the parson and the bosses. But the very fact that ordination is seen as something of a sacrifice shows the low social status of the occupation. The respect is at arm's length; it is a good thing that there are people like that, but we do not want to be like them.

Although clerics no longer receive their income in farm produce, much of it still comes 'in kind': most denominations provide their officials with housing and transport and meet such costs as telephone bills. It is thus a little difficult to make accurate comparisons. We also need to remember that for every cleric like Trollope's wealthy Archdeacon Grantly there were three or four like poor Mr Quiverful, barely subsisting and falling a long way short of the gentlemanly standard of living that was implied. In *A Clergyman's Daughter*, George Orwell depicts perfectly the world of gentile lower-middle-class poverty. But what is incontrovertible is that, as the standards of living of the general working population have risen (real income doubled between 1949 and 1978), clergy incomes, though narrowing in range, have fallen behind. The Church of England's own figures show that between 1972 and 1994 the retail price index (the commonly used mark of inflation) went from 100 to 122, and average earnings moved ahead of it, but the average clergy stipend went down from 100 to 77.

The Godly People

Even within the Christian tradition, there are considerable differences in what counts as a 'member'. Seeing themselves as having a mission to a whole population, the Roman Catholic Church and the Church of England traditionally counted all those whom they baptized. At the other extreme we find sectarian Protestant organizations such as the Free Presbyterian Church of Scotland where people may attend conscientiously all their lives and still not feel sufficiently sure of their 'calling' to ask to be admitted as full members. With various adjustments to compensate for most differences within denominations, we can estimate the present proportion of the adult population of the United Kingdom which 'belongs' to the Christian churches as about 14 per cent, or 6.7 million people. Three-quarters of these are members of just three denominations: the Church of England, the Church of Scotland, and the Catholic Church.

All the major Protestant denominations have lost members this century. Table 2.2 shows the lay members of the Church of England at various points from 1900 to 1990. Although the total rises in the first half of the century, as we can see from the third column, it fails to keep pace with population growth, and then it declines in absolute numbers to just over half of what it was at the start of century. Assessing Methodist membership is slightly more difficult because at the start of the century English Methodism was divided, but, as we see in the amalgamated figures in Table 2.3, it shows a similar picture.

The same can be found in the membership figures for the Church of Scotland. If one takes the 1900 figure as the base of 100, membership increases to 110 in 1920, fluctuates around that until 1960, and then falls rapidly to 69 in 1990. But again, more revealing than the total of members is the degree of community penetration. In order to keep

Table 2.2 Church of England Membership, 1900–1990

Year	Members (000s)	Ratio	% of adult population
1900	2,800	100	13.5
1930	3,100	131	12.8
1950	3,000	106	9.2
1970	2,600	92	7.2
1990	1,500	55	3.9

Source: Peter Brierley, A Century of British Christianity: Historical Statistics 1900–1985 with Projections to 2000 (Research Monograph 14; London: MARC Europe, 1989).

Table 2.3 Methodist Membership, England, 1900–1990

Year	Members (000s)	Ratio	% of adult population
1900	727	100	3.1
1930	788	109	2.5
1950	682	97	2.0
1970	572	80	1.5
1990	416	57	1.0

Source: As for Table 2.2.

Table 2.4 Roman Catholics, Britain, 1900–1990

Year	England and Wales		Scotland		Britain		
	Total (m.)	Ratio	Total (m.)	Ratio	Total (m.)	Ratio	% of total population
1900	1.6	100	0.5	100	2.0	100	5.5
1930	2.2	139	0.6	129	2.8	137	6.2
1950	2.8	176	0.7	159	3.5	172	7.2
1970	4.1	263	0.8	175	4.9	242	9.1
1990	4.3	271	0.8	175	5.1	249	9.1

Source: As for Table 2.2.

pace with population growth, the Kirk should have grown by 13 per cent. Instead, it has declined by a third. Furthermore, it is clear from the age profile of members that the growth in the middle of the century owed more to existing members living longer than to new members being recruited.

Adding the experience of other major denominations confirms this general decline. The Calvinistic Methodists in Wales (latterly known as the Presbyterian Church of Wales) grew from 158,000 in 1900 to a peak of 189,000 in 1925 and then declined to about 63,000 in 1990. The proportion of British people who were Baptists fell from 1.4 per cent in 1900 to 0.5 per cent in 1990.

We can bring together the membership figures for all the Christian denominations and chart the overall pattern. To make Protestant and Catholic data comparable, I have used the numbers attending mass on an average Sunday for the Catholic totals for 1970 and 1990. What Table 2.5 and Figure 2.1 show is a remorseless decline relative to the adult population.

Table 2.5 Christian Church Membership, Britain, 1900–1990

Year	All Protestant	Roman Catholic	All Christian		
	Total (m.)	Total (m.)	Total (m.)	Ratio	% of adult population
1900	5.4	2.0	7.4	100	30
1930	7.1	2.8	9.9	133	29
1950	6.1	3.5	9.6	129	25
1970	5.2	2.7	7.9	107	19
1990	3.4	2.2	5.6	76	12

Note: For comparability, the 1970 and 1990 Catholic figures are for mass attendance on an average Sunday. As the proportion of 'observant' Catholics has steadily declined over the century from over 80% to less than 40%, 1900, 1930, and 1950 data have been left as the total Catholic population. If they had also been adjusted, the decline in percentage of total adult population who are church members would be slightly but not significantly less dramatic.

Sources: Peter Brierley, *A Century of British Christianity: Historical Statistics 1900–1985 with Projections to 2000* (Research Monograph 14; London: MARC Europe, 1989); Robert Currie, Alan D. Gilbert, and Lee Horsley, *Churches and Churchgoers: Patterns of Church Growth in the British Isles since 1700* (Oxford: Oxford University Press, 1977); Peter Brierley and Val Hiscock, *UK Christian Handbook 1994/95 edition* (London: Christian Research Association, 1993).

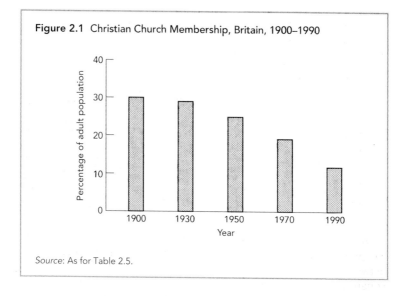

Figure 2.1 Christian Church Membership, Britain, 1900–1990

Source: As for Table 2.5.

Church Attendance

As we might suppose that it takes more effort to attend church than to remain a church member, it is worth comparing attendance and membership. The Roman Catholic problem has already been mentioned. However, the relationship is reversed for the more conservative Protestant sects and denominations. A Scottish survey in 1984 expressed attendance as a percentage of members and produced the figures in Table 2.6, which show the small and conservative Protestant sects and denominations attracting more people to their services than actually belong and very large numbers of people claiming to be members of the main churches but not darkening their doors.

There is no one reliable way of measuring church-going. It is prohibitively expensive to place enumerators outside a sufficiently large number of churches to be sure that their counting is representative. So we either survey a sample of the general public and ask them how often they go to church or we ask clergymen to estimate the size of their congregations. The general survey has the weakness that respondents may exaggerate their church-going as they give what they feel are the expected answers. Contrary to what we might expect, priests, ministers, and pastors do not exaggerate their popularity. When researchers have

Table 2.6 Church Attendance as a Proportion of Members, Scotland, 1984 (%)

Baptist	107
Independent churches	76
Other denominations	75
Free/Free Presbyterian/Reformed Presbyterian	68
Scottish Episcopal	40
Roman Catholic	35
Church of Scotland	29

Source: Peter Brierley and Fergus Macdonald, *Prospects for Scotland: From a Census of the Churches in 1984* (Edinburgh: The Bible Society of Scotland, 1985).

set out to elicit claims of attendance in surveys and test them against clergy estimates, they have found the survey data overestimating by between 50 and 100 per cent. However, there is the danger that some congregations (especially of new or small denominations) will be over-looked when we are collecting clergy estimates. The organizer of the 1989 English Church Census, Peter Brierley, admits that the independent evangelical groups (often still called 'house churches', although most are too big to meet in houses) are under-represented in that study, but a generous allowance would give only an additional 40,000 adults in 800 groups, which would not alter the basic conclusions.

As we see in Table 2.7, fewer than one in ten people in England attend church and they are fairly evenly divided between the state Church of England, the Roman Catholic Church, and the various Nonconformist denominations. The largest of those was the Methodists with just under

Table 2.7 Church Attendance, England, 1989

Nonconformist	1.25 m.
Church of England	1.14 m.
Roman Catholic	1.30 m.
Total Christian	3.71 m.
Total adult population	38.83 m.
Adult church attenders as % of adult population	9.55%

Source: Peter Brierley, *'Christian' England: What the English Church Census Reveals* (London: MARC Europe, 1991).

400,000, then the various independent Protestant churches (292,000), the Baptists (199,000), and the United Reformed Church (114,000).

The 1989 English Church Census had been preceded by one in 1979 and both asked clergy to estimate their congregations four years earlier. A similar survey was conducted in Scotland in 1984. If we add the figures from Horace Mann's 1851 Census of Religious Worship[2] and some 1959 figures, we get the trajectory of Figure 2.2.

In many European settings we find the pattern of the regions and peripheries being more orthodox in their religion than the metropolitan centres. In part this is a matter of the edges of an economy being less touched by such secularizing forces as industrialization, but part of the difference is explained by the deliberate reaction of the peripheries to the secular nature of the centre. One of the ways in which some Scottish, Welsh, and Ulster people express their identity is through continued allegiance to their own more conservative and rigorous Protestant traditions. Within each of those countries, the centre-

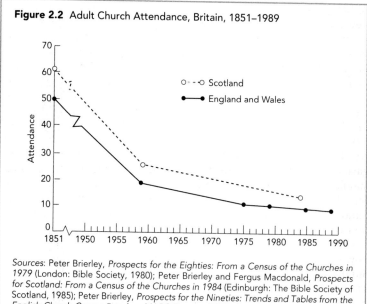

Figure 2.2 Adult Church Attendance, Britain, 1851–1989

Sources: Peter Brierley, *Prospects for the Eighties: From a Census of the Churches in 1979* (London: Bible Society, 1980); Peter Brierley and Fergus Macdonald, *Prospects for Scotland: From a Census of the Churches in 1984* (Edinburgh: The Bible Society of Scotland, 1985); Peter Brierley, *Prospects for the Nineties: Trends and Tables from the English Church Census* (London: MARC Europe, 1991); British Parliamentary Papers, *1851 Census, Great Britain, Report and Tables on Religious Worship 1852–3* (repr. Irish University Press, 1970); British Parliamentary Papers, *Religious Worship and Education, Scotland, Report and Tables* (London: HMSO, 1854).

periphery difference is repeated. In Scotland the highest rates of church attendance are found in the Highlands and Islands and the lowest rates in the industrial lowlands. However, with improvements in transport and mass communication the distinctiveness of the edges is declining as they become incorporated into the national and international culture.

An additional factor in the Scottish case is the greater presence of the Catholic Church. As was noted in Chapter One, the Catholic Church used to benefit from its additional social role as the institutional centre of a migrant minority. As the descendants of the Irish in Scotland have become more thoroughly assimilated, so the distinctively high rate of mass attendance has declined towards the Protestant norm. Hence the rapid decline in Scottish church attendance.

Sunday Schools

Although they were never entirely successful as structures for recruiting new members, the Sunday schools run by the Christian churches were a vital point of contact between formal religion and the mass of the people. In the nineteenth century they were extremely popular, in part because they provided an alternative source of basic education for people who did not want to lose the labour of their children during the working week. Along with ancillary organizations such as choirs, youth clubs, and the Boys' Brigade, Sunday schools with their outings and picnics also offered one of the main sources of leisure activity. Richard Hoggart, describing working-class culture in the 1950s, talked of 'the steadiness with which children are enrolled in Sunday School'.[3] He gave as the main reason for it the parents' desire that their children should be instructed, not so much in 'religion' but in ethics and morals, but also pointed to the secondary appeals of giving parents a quiet Sunday afternoon with their children out of the cramped terraced houses of the industrial towns.

That has now gone. Whereas the Church of England's membership now stands at just under 50 per cent of its 1900 value, the number of Sunday-school pupils is less than 10 per cent of its 1900 value, and the same trajectory can be seen in all the major denominations for which figures are available. Whereas the turn-of-the-century Sunday school provided a service which was used by the community far beyond the congregation that provided it, the modern Sunday school is attended only by the children of members. The shorter working week, better housing, and smaller families have given adults more leisure time and reduced the need for temporary relief from the noisy presence of their offspring. There is now greater expectation that parents will do interesting things with their children rather than farm them out. One has to suppose, though, that non-church-goers do not send their children to Sunday school because they no longer believe that the church or chapel is the right place for moral and ethical education.

The Social Composition of Church-goers

As outlined in Chapter One, religion in pre-Reformation Europe was a combination of three things: a church which performed official religion on behalf of the whole people, a very widely diffused but not terribly well-informed Christian faith, and a pervasive superstitious belief in the supernatural. The fragmentation of that religious culture often proceeded along class and regional lines, and, in each location and period, sects and denominations tended to have a distinctive social identity. As formal involvement in structured religion declined, that decline seemed to affect some classes and regions more than others. Although this depiction misses some of the detail, in general, despite the success of nineteenth-century evangelical sects in recruiting from the top of the new urban working class, the least religious people were those closest to industrial production: working-class adult males living in towns and cities.

What is known about the social characteristics of contemporary church-goers? First, they tend to be women. Whereas the sexes are pretty evenly balanced in the general population (51 per cent female to 49 per cent male), 63 per cent of Scottish church attenders in 1984 were women. Of English church attenders in 1979, 55 per cent were women; in 1989, it was 58 per cent. An even clearer pattern emerges if one separates different levels of attendance: as Table 2.8 shows, almost two-thirds of frequent church-goers in Britain and Northern Ireland are women.

Figure 2.3 graphically shows the skewing of the age profile to the young and the old. In Scotland 25 per cent of church-goers are under 15, as against 21 per cent in the general population. Twenty-four per cent of church-goers are aged 45–64 compared with 22 per cent in the general population. The English pattern is much the same. When one combines the age and gender profiles, one concludes that young men are not very interested in institutional religion.

It is relatively easy to ascertain or guess someone's age and guessing gender should cause no great problem. But class can really only be measured through surveys which ask respondents about their occupa-

Table 2.8 Gender and Church Attendance, Britain and Northern Ireland, 1991 (%)

Attendance	Britain		Northern Ireland	
	Men	Women	Men	Women
Frequent	37	63	39	61
Regular	35	65	57	43
Rare	48	52	49	51

Source: 1991 British Social Attitudes Survey.

Figure 2.3 Church Attendance, by Age, England (1991) and Scotland (1984)

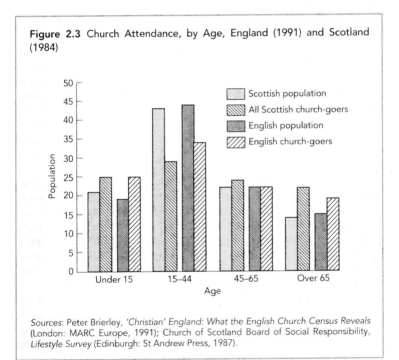

Sources: Peter Brierley, *'Christian' England: What the English Church Census Reveals* (London: MARC Europe, 1991); Church of Scotland Board of Social Responsibility, *Lifestyle Survey* (Edinburgh: St Andrew Press, 1987).

tions and their church-going habits. As such surveys are relatively recent in Britain, we do not have the data with which to make historical comparisons, but we know that there is presently a class factor in church-going.

As Table 2.9 shows, 16 per cent of white-collar and professional people questioned in 1991 said they went to church at least once a fortnight while only 12 per cent of manual workers made the same claim, and there are matching differences in the proportions who said they never went to church. The same survey shows a very similar link between education and church-going. Graduates and others with experience of higher education are more likely than expected to be frequent church attenders, while those with no qualifications are more likely to attend 'never'.

Table 2.9 Social Class and Church Attendance, Britain, 1991 (%)

Attendance	Non-manual	Manual
Fortnightly or more	16	12
Monthly–once a year	29	24
Less than once a year	3	4
Never	48	57
No answer	3	3

Source: 1991 British Social Attitudes Survey.

Even when they are conducted by the same organization not too many years apart, surveys rarely ask questions or code responses in an identical manner, and we must be wary of taking differing survey results as evidence of actual change in the absence of other good evidence. Commentators writing in the 1950s and 1960s reported that church-going was strongly influenced by gender, age, and class. My analysis of the 1991 British Social Attitudes Survey data, which contain the responses of over 2,000 people, often produced relationships that were, to describe them technically, 'statistically significant' but with 'weak associations'. It may well be that the way the questions were asked and the responses coded has obscured strong associations, but I rather suspect that the statistical problems provide an illuminating metaphor for a real change. In rejecting certain associations as unreliable because there were too few cases, the statistical procedures were inadvertently making the main point: church attendance has now become so rare in Britain that it is no longer supported by group pressure and is no longer an important mark of 'belonging' to any larger social formation. It has become an almost purely personal or idiosyncratic matter.

Nostalgic Images

All of the above data point to institutional decay, but we would be missing something important if we stopped after concluding that this century has seen a steady decrease in the size, popularity, and influence of the major Christian denominations. Consider the popular images of rural England. Beside the village green, there stands the church. In the flat fields of Lincolnshire, the towers of ancient Saxon and Norman buildings are often the only visible landmark. Phillip Larkin's sombre 'Church Going' ('wondering, too | When churches fall completely out of use | What we shall turn them into . . .') gives a good sense of decay, but John Betjeman's better-known 'Summoned by Bells' shows a fondness for churches that reminds us of the place that a stylized Edwardian church has in images of England. Consider how often vicars and vicarages appear in the crime fiction of Agatha Christie, Dorothy L. Sayers, or Ngaio Marsh. As part of our general nostalgic appreciation of those period pieces, we continue to consume cultural products in which the church is an important part of the social landscape.

We could say the same of the place of the dissenting chapel and its male voice choir in images of Wales. Or consider the 'Kirk' in Scottish perceptions of Scottishness. That it was one of the few Scottish institutions left after the Union of Scotland and England made it a cornerstone of Scottishness, but it was also held to exemplify particularly Scottish virtues: a little stuffy, but learned and democratic. For those two reasons it has a place in the affections of very many Scots who never feel moved to occupy its pews. In the 1950s church leaders keen on closer union with the Church of England proposed, as the price for full intercommunion with the English church, that the Kirk adopt something of the episcopal style by having each Presbytery elect a bishop, and in so doing ran into a barrage of flak. With the full backing of the owner of the Express newspaper group, Lord Beaverbrook (a Canadian millionaire who liked to remember that he was the son of a Scottish Presbyterian minister), the *Scottish Daily Express* launched a massive campaign against the 'Bishops in Presbytery' proposals. Pamphlets entitled *Crisis in the Kirk* and *The Crux of the Matter* were printed in runs of thousands and given away at the *Express*'s expense. The scheme was rejected by the Kirk's General Assembly, but through the 1960s the *Express* continued to take a close interest in church matters and to present itself as a defender of a distinctive Scottish institution under threat, not just from liberal Christians, but from the English and from the Edinburgh bourgeoisie who could not be trusted with the safe-keeping of Scotland's jewels. What the *Express*'s interest showed was that many Scots with little or no formal connection to the church still regarded the Kirk as a national asset to be treasured and revered, if not actively supported by participation.

The major denominations are no longer able to command the specific allegiances of many people, but their historic presence is such that they retain the status of icons. The regard may be nostalgic and it may be annoying to committed Christians. In 'Church Going' Larkin asks 'if we shall keep | A few cathedrals chronically on show | Their parchment, plate and pyx in locked cases'. The religious professionals who have to keep the great English cathedrals on show are reasonably infuriated by the mass of non-church-goers who do nothing to contribute to their enormous costs but who complain when charged entrance fees. Committed activists want the church's diminishing resources directed to promoting the church's mission today, but many outside the churches want the buildings retained as monuments whose offices can be consumed when it suits: primarily for carol-singing at Christmas. None the less, the fondness for the visible symbols of the history of the Christian churches should not be dismissed as socially meaningless; it is not. The association of England and the Church of England can lead to some bizarre conclusions, as in the example of the atheist who was committed to religious education on the grounds that to remove it would allow members of ethnic minorities to avoid an important part of what should be required of a loyal citizen: 'I think this trouble over teaching religion in schools is a disgrace. Our religion is Church of England. If we went abroad I bet we'd have to accept their religion.'[4] In less confrontational form, the supposition that 'our religion is Church of England' (and its regional equivalents) is shared by many people long outside formal religion and it is testimony to the distinctive history of secularization in Britain: institutional religion eroded by indifference rather than confronted by hostility. The church may be going, but it will be fondly missed by a large body of people wistful for things past.

Religion beyond the Churches

All religions involve shared rituals even if, as in the case of the Quakers, those rituals are specified in no more detail than gathering in a certain place at a certain time and waiting on the Holy Spirit or Inner Light to move you to say something, or lead in a prayer, or suggest a song. Even those variants of Protestantism that are firmly opposed to 'ritual' encourage people to join together in some enduring way so that they can remind each other why they are opposed to ritual. It is thus no accident that religions are 'carried' or embodied by religious organizations. None the less we can imagine a lack of overlap between being 'religious' and 'being involved with a religious institution' at both ends of the stick. Some people's reasons for being involved with a church are mundane: the landowner who feels obliged to 'give a lead' in his community or the woman who does the flower-arranging because she likes to feel of some value. At the other end there may well be people who think of themselves as deeply religious and who spend considerable time communing with God but who feel alienated from the available religious institutions.

Clearly church involvement is not the only expression of religion nor is it a necessary one. We cannot immediately assume that because we are far less likely than our grandparents to be church-goers ours is a less religious society. Many Christians interpret the decline of the churches as an expression of the modern lack of faith in institutions of any sort, rather than as a lack of faith. There is an obvious weakness in that proposition. Imagine someone tells you that he is a big football fan. You ask if he is a member of a supporters' club and he says not. You ask which team he supports and he is unsure. You ask when he last went to a match and he says he has not been for twenty years. He also admits that he never reads reports of games in the papers, changes channels when football comes on the television, cannot name any prominent footballers, and never plays himself. At some point in this inquisition it becomes clear that 'football fan' is here being used in an unusual manner. The claim that a significant number of those Britons who are not involved in any of the vast range of religious activities that are on offer are none the less 'religious' is open to the same objection. We also need to be cautious of too readily accepting those reasons for not going to church which deflect attention from faith. Assertions that 'I'm too busy' and 'the services are boring' need to be understood in context. We have far more leisure time and far less tiring jobs than our ancestors and, unlike the case in the Middle Ages, services are at least conducted in a language we understand! Clergymen who think that acoustic guitars will draw in the unchurched are rather missing the point. When the committed football fan will stand in the cold and rain for two hours every Saturday to watch his team, we have to suspect that those who explain their lack of church involvement by considerations other than a lack of belief are fooling themselves or fooling the researchers.

But rather than dismiss as naïve the notion that the unchurched are not ungodly, we can try to discover just what those outside the churches believe. The first and most honest thing to say is that such investigation is fraught with technical problems. Other than by seeing people act on a certain belief or opinion, we can only discern what they think or feel by asking them. In order to ask a large enough number of people to be confident that the answers are representative of a large social group, we need to use the prestructured question-and-answer format of the social survey and we are well aware of the weaknesses in data generated by such instruments. I have already mentioned the known gulf between what people claim to be their pattern of church attendance and the actual pattern of church-going. Even if we assume that respondents are really doing their best to give accurate and truthful answers to questions, we still have the problem of having to believe that all respondents interpret our questions in the same way and mean the same thing by their answers. Generally speaking, the more concrete the issue, the more reliable the response. Surveys are better at discovering the ownership of televisions or inside toilets than they are at discerning attitudes, and the more abstract the issue at stake the less useful the data. Asking people if they agree with the government's privatization of the water supply will produce more reliable responses than asking if they believe in God. None the less, surveys have asked people if they believe in God, if they are religious, and so on, and, provided we are careful in the conclusions we draw from them, such data are worth reporting.

What Do We Believe?

A consistent finding of such surveys is that a very high proportion of people in Britain assert a denominational identification. Generally less than a quarter of respondents in a variety of surveys claim 'no religion'. To be more specific, few people claim to be atheists or agnostics. As we see in Table 2.10, in the 1991 British Social Attitudes Survey only 10 per cent claim to be atheists (position 1) and 13 per cent gave the agnostic answer (position 2). However, the unbelievers are now more numerous than a decade earlier, when only 4 per cent identified themselves as 'atheists'. Further information about those atheists shows the difficulties in making inferences from such data. Of the forty-five who asserted that there is no God, twenty also claimed a denominational attachment, ten believed in some sort of spirit or life force, ten believed in life after death, and one believed in a personal God! That neatly mirrors the confusion identified in a 1940s Mass Observation survey of a London Borough which noted that: 'Of the doubters, agnostics and atheists . . .

over a quarter say they pray on occasions to the God whose existence they doubt. One in twelve went to church within the past six months, compared with one in three of those who say they believe in God. Over half of the non-believers consider there should be religious education in schools.'[5] However ambivalent and inconsistent the unbelievers, the history of post-war surveys is one of increasing unbelief. In 1947 only 6 per cent said, to use the Gallup formula, that they 'Don't really think there is any sort of spirit/God or life force'; in 1968 it was 11 per cent.

Table 2.10 Belief in God, Britain and Northern Ireland, 1991

	Position	Britain (%)	Northern Ireland (%)
'I don't believe in God'	1	10	1
'I don't know whether there is a God and I don't believe there is any way to find out'	2	14	4
'I don't believe in a personal God but I do believe in a higher power of some kind'	3	13	4
'I find myself believing in God some of the time but not at others'	4	13	7
'While I have doubts, I feel that I do believe in God'	5	26	20
'I know God really exists and I have no doubts about it'	6	23	57
'I don't know' and 'No answer'	7	2	7

Source: 1991 British Social Attitudes Survey.

Secondly, and this is not just a restatement of the previous point, most people say they believe in some sort of God. Table 2.10 shows 75 per cent claiming to believe in some sort of supernatural power (positions 3–6). The picture is muddied somewhat by the questions running together what people believe and how sure they are of such beliefs, but at first glance there is a lot of God about.

But just how important is that God? The 1991 British Social Attitudes Survey asked about 'closeness to God' and in typical survey form gave four options: not close at all, not very close, somewhat close, and extremely close. Half the sample believed in God but only half of those felt close to God and almost a quarter felt 'not close at all'.

The survey also asked about changes in belief, and two things are worth noting about the answers (see Table 2.11). A full quarter of the sample could not or would not choose an answer. And those who had once believed but no longer did outnumbered by two to one those who had become believers.

With all the usual cautions about comparability, we can put side-by-side the results of a number of surveys which confronted respondents with a choice between the traditional Christian view of God as a person and an alternative which could encompass a very wide range of non-theistic visions of the supernatural. The results are given in Table 2.12 and they show the Christian version to be the minority one. The majority of those who think there is more to life than meets the eye no longer accept the traditional teachings of the Christian churches. To take the

Table 2.11 Reported Changes in Belief, Britain, 1991 (%)

'I don't believe in God now and never have'	12
'I don't believe in God now but I used to'	12
'I believe in God now but I didn't used to'	6
'I believe in God now and I always have'	46
'I can't choose' and 'No answer'	25

Source: 1991 British Social Attitudes Survey.

Table 2.12 'What is God?' Britain, 1947–1987 (%)

	1947	1957	1987
'There is a personal God'	45	41	37
'There is some sort of spirit or vital force which controls life'	39	37	42
'I am not sure that there is any sort of God or life force'	16	—	—
'I don't know what to think'	—	16	—
'I don't really think there is any sort of spirit/god or life force'	—	6	—
'Don't know', other, or neither	—	—	21

Sources: George H. Gallup (ed.), *The Gallup International Public Opinion Polls; Great Britain 1937–1975* (New York: Random House, 1976); Michael Svennevig, Ian Haldane, Sharon Speirs, and Barrie Gunter, *Godwatching: Viewers, Religion and Television* (London: John Libbey/IBA, 1989).

central Christian claim, 71 per cent of Gallup respondents in 1951 agreed that 'Jesus Christ is the Son of God'. In 1965 it was 64 per cent and in 1982 it was only 43 per cent. Further evidence of the lessening popularity of what were once core Christian beliefs is given in Table 2.13 which reports four sets of responses to fundamental religious beliefs.

When we put these observations together with the evidence of decline in the popularity of the churches, we can see an increasingly secular people gradually losing faith in the specific teachings of the Christian tradition but retaining a fondness for vague religious affirmations. While it leaves out of the picture for the time being those people from a non-Christian culture (they were only about 2 per cent of the 1991 survey sample), one way of thinking about the ranges of belief tapped by surveys is to envisage a series of circles which represent such attitudes as 'believing in God', 'praying frequently', and 'thinking of oneself as religious'. In the centre of the area where these related attitudes most overlap, we have the committed Christians, but we also have considerable numbers in parts of the circles that do not overlap. For example, while there is the expected association between traditional belief in God and thinking of oneself as religious, a quarter of the atheists and agnostics choose the neutral option rather than the expected 'non-religious' label. While those who attend church frequently are most likely to see themselves as religious people, lots of the unchurched also describe themselves as 'religious'. Although there is the expected and clear statistical connection between seeing oneself as religious and how often one prays, there is a large proportion (29 per cent) of people who call themselves religious but rarely pray.

Table 2.13 Beliefs, Britain, 1957–1991 (%)

	1957	1981	1987	1991
Sin	—	69	51	—
Soul	—	59	50	—
Heaven	—	57	48	46
Life after death	54	45	43	27
Devil	34	30	31	24
Hell	—	27	29	24

Sources: George H. Gallup (ed.), The Gallup International Public Opinion Polls; Great Britain 1937–1975 (New York: Random House, 1976); David Gerard, 'Religious Attitudes and Values', in Mark Abrams, David Gerard, and Noel Timms, Values and Social Change in Britain (London: Macmillan, 1985), 50–92; Michael Svennevig, Ian Haldane, Sharon Speirs, and Barrie Gunter, Godwatching: Viewers, Religion and Television (London: John Libbey/IBA, 1989); 1991 British Social Attitudes Survey.

The Social Correlates of Belief

Exploring the social characteristics of those who give certain responses to general religious-attitude questions shows some continuities with what we know of church-goers, but, not surprisingly, the patterns are generally weaker and sometimes they are entirely absent.

Age is a major determinant of seeing oneself as religious (see Table 2.14), but there is no clear link with gender. There are links between self-description as 'religious' and levels of education, income, or social class, but they are weaker than those found for church attendance and *they run in the opposite direction*. In Table 2.15 two numbers are given for each category: the actual total in that category and, below to the right in italics, the number we would expect if the respondents were simply allocated to each category according to its size. If there is a big difference between the actual and expected figures, then we probably have a connection which is not accidental. Social class I people, the professionals and senior management, are less likely than expected to describe themselves as religious; unskilled manual workers more so. A similar pattern can be found in the relationship between income and changes in belief in God. If we take an annual income of £15,000 as the line around which we divide the sample, we can note that the most popular response—always believed in God—is given by 63 per cent of those below that line and only 55 per cent of those above it. Only 15 per cent of those below but 19 per cent of those above said they had never believed in God. There was also markedly more loss of faith (those who 'did believe once, but do not now') among the better off.

What these data seem to show is that the middle classes are much more decisive in their religious behaviour and narrow in their use of terms to describe it. More middle-class than working-class people are involved with the churches, but those who are not are less likely than

Table 2.14 Age and Religious Self-Image, Britain, 1991 (%)

Self-image	Age		
	18–24	25–59	60 plus
Religious	26	37	60
Undecided	31	35	25
Non-religious	42	28	14

Source: 1991 British Social Attitudes Survey.

Table 2.15 Social Class and Religious Self-Image, Britain, 1991

Self-image	Social Class					
	Non-manual			Manual		
	I Professional	II Intermediate	III Routine	III Skilled	IV Partly skilled	V Unskilled
Religious	18	107	138	96	78	41
Expect	*25*	*117*	*116*	*101*	*82*	*36*
Undecided	23	99	71	81	75	23
Expect	*20*	*91*	*90*	*79*	*64*	*28*
Non-religious	19	78	70	68	46	24
Expect	*16*	*75*	*74*	*65*	*52*	*23*

Source: 1991 British Social Attitudes Survey.

their working-class counterparts to claim religious beliefs or describe themselves as religious. In his rich description of working-class life before and after the war, Hoggart makes the point that the word 'Christian' was used to mean decent, charitable, ethical, and moral; that is, to describe what were taken to be the behavioural residues of the Christian faith rather than the faith itself. I suspect something similar is going on with the word 'religious' in contemporary surveys. A recent study by Barrie Gunter and Rachel Vinney which complemented the conventional survey with focused group discussions showed many respondents taking a very practical view of religion. One person said 'religion without rules is not religion'. The authors very neatly summarized what they thought their respondents valued by saying that they were keen on the last six of the ten commandments. The specifically religious requirements—have no other gods before me, make no graven images, do not take the Lord's name in vain, and keep the Sabbath holy—have gone and the valued state of being 'religious' now means not killing, not committing adultery, not stealing, not lying, and not being covetous. Though few people now believe in the God who was the source of these principles for good living, the principles themselves—or even just the idea of having principles—are still respected. In 1951, 69 per cent of respondents said that it was important for religious instruction to be given in schools. One might have expected forty years of secularization to have diminished that desire, but, in the 1991 survey, 64 per cent said that there should 'definitely' or 'probably' be daily prayers in schools against 27 per cent who thought not.

Most people in Britain are not connected to the churches, do not subscribe to the core beliefs of the religion that shaped their culture, and are rather suspicious of those who take religion 'too seriously' and who have 'got God'. Yet most people like the idea of religion and are keen to have some taught to their children (though not keen enough to send them to Sunday school!).

The Supernatural

We can move even further from the Christian tradition and consider what, if any, beliefs about the supernatural, conceived most generally, are held by the British people. There is certainly plenty of superstition about. In one large 1976 survey 36 per cent of people said they had been 'aware of, or influenced by a presence or power, whether referred to as God or not, which is different from their everyday lives'.[6] The 1991 Social Attitudes Survey offered the propositions listed in Table 2.16 and produced a considerable amount of assent to views that are incompatible with a rational and materialist model of causation. The respondents were also asked if they had ever been in touch with the dead. Sixty-three per cent said 'never', 17 per cent said 'one or twice', 8 per

Table 2.16 Superstitions, Britain, 1991 (%)

Propositions	'Definitely' and 'Probably' true	'Probably' and 'Definitely' false	'I can't choose' and 'No answer'
Good luck charms sometimes do bring good luck	22	72	6
Some fortune-tellers really can foresee the future	40	53	8
Some faith-healers really do have God-given healing powers	45	45	10
A person's star sign at birth, or horoscope, can affect the course of their future	28	64	9

Source: 1991 British Social Attitudes Survey.

cent answered 'several times' or 'often', and 12 per cent could not say. A surprisingly large proportion—half of those who gave an answer—said they believed in the possibility of faith-healing.

Which of these statistics is noteworthy rather depends on the implicit comparison. What is clear is that the decline in traditional Christianity is not to be explained by saying that modern people, the beneficiaries of science and technology, are incapable of believing in the supernatural. However, if one compares these sorts of figures with what we know of people in pre-modern societies, it is clear that the supernatural is much less of a presence. If we go back to the 1976 survey, we can note, not the impressive 36 per cent who claimed some sort of supernatural experience, but the group that is almost twice as large: those who said they had 'never' had such an experience. Compare that with the medieval world of charms, amulets, spells, shrines with magical powers, holy waters for the protection of houses and beasts, holy relics, bones of the apostles, and pieces of the original cross, and we see how much more secular is our world.

Religious Broadcasting

Another possible indicator of religious interest outside the churches is the audience for religious broadcasting. Since the creation of first radio and then television, the British electronic media have always given a privileged position to the churches. The first director of the British Broadcasting Company (later Corporation), John Reith, was a devout Presbyterian Scot who ensured that the voice of Christianity was clearly and frequently heard on the new medium.

In comparison with the American product, British religious broadcasting is immensely staid. Where televangelists in the United States preach their distinctive gospel, criticize those who disagree with them, and attempt to recruit followers for their particular brand, British religious broadcasting early on established itself as ecumenical, denominational, tolerant, and uncontroversial, and, although the 1990 Broadcasting Act in many other respects opened up the electronic media to free-market principles, it fixed as a legal requirement the British understanding of what was acceptable in religious programming. In the American model individuals or particular sects produce their own programmes, buy air time to show them, and appeal to their audiences for funds to purchase more air time. In the British system the television companies give air time free, and opportunities to broadcast are generally rotated around the denominations roughly in proportion to their size. Until recently, religion departments of television companies generally recruited producers to represent the major Christian traditions. So, if there were three producers, one would be a Catholic priest, one an Anglican vicar, and one a Nonconformist minister.

In the days when there were relatively few radio and television channels, religious programmes were very popular, especially if they featured hymn-singing. The Methodist movement pioneered the use of sentimental lyrics set to simple folk tunes as the core of communal worship and as the main vehicle for teaching people their faith. The subsequent evangelical revival in the Church of England and the popularity of the songs brought to Victorian Britain by American evangelists such as Moody and Sankey so firmly established the place of hymn-singing that a historian could write: 'If there has been a common religion in England in the last hundred years, it has been based not on doctrine but on popular hymns'[7] and the same could be said of the rest of the United Kingdom. Until 1993 BBC1 and ITV simultaneously transmitted music-based religious programmes in the Sunday evening 6.40–7.10 p.m. prime-time 'God slot'. In that scheduling format, the BBC's *Songs of Praise* and ITV's *Stars on Sunday* and its successor *Highway* attracted something like 60 per cent of the audience. But before we take this as evidence of massive extra-church interest in religion, we should note that what appears to be evidence of popularity is in the first instance only a measure of presence. If two of the four terrestrial channels show a religious programme and the audience was entirely neutral about the appeal of those programmes, they would attract 50 per cent of the audience!

Though large, the audiences have steadily declined. In the late 1970s, ITV's *Stars on Sunday* was watched by between 12 and 15 million people (which was about 75 per cent of the audience for the most popular programme, *Coronation Street*). Its successor *Highway* attracted 7.8 million viewers in 1987 and 7 million in 1992. The BBC's *Songs of Praise*, essentially an outside broadcast of a church service, was watched by almost 7 million people in 1987 and between 5 and 5.5 million in 1992. Because audience size and share is in the first place a function, not of demand, but of supply, audience researchers have used surveys to gauge demand, and their conclusion is stark:

The 1968 survey showed that 40 per cent of respondents deliberately turned on to watch a religious programme and over half said they paid attention when a religious programme was on. By 1987, this was found to have changed, with only seven per cent of people saying they deliberately turned on when a religious programme was being shown.[8]

However popular they were, the music-based programmes that traditionally occupied the 'God slot' were not liked by the people who determined TV schedules because they attracted the wrong sort of audience. Typical viewers could not be relied on to stay with that channel for the rest of the evening (the aim of the schedulers), but worse, for the commercial channels, they were the wrong sort of people. Although most viewers saw the main purpose of religious broadcasting as 'the provision of services for people who cannot get to church'[9] the audience was heavily biased towards church-goers and towards the demographic groups from which church-goers were drawn—the elderly and the female—and they were not terribly receptive to inducements to buy expensive cars and foreign holidays. Throughout the 1980s, programmers pressed for the fixed 'God slot' to be abandoned. At first they were repelled by pressure from church leaders, but in 1993 the ITV television executives won and religious broadcasting was switched out of its preserved prime-time space.

Although the most recent legislation still requires broadcasters to feature religion, an increasing proportion of 'religious' programmes are being made by broadcasters with an interest in religion rather than clergymen with an interest in broadcasting. And that interest is often academic rather than personal. So the religion output (the BBC's *Everyman* or *Heart of the Matter* would be examples) has come to be more about religion and less religious.

While the changing nature of religious broadcasting and its declining popularity are obviously part of the general process of secularization, some of the decline has been caused by increased competition. When *Songs of Praise* was becoming established as a venerable British institution, there were only two television channels. There are now four and additional alternatives in the form of cable, satellite, and video. When satellite first became available, many liberal churchmen feared that we would see the introduction of aggressive proselytizing 'holy-roller' televangelism, but this has not yet happened. A 1991 survey showed that very few people were aware that programmes such as Robert Schuller's *Hour of Power* and *Victory with Morris Cerullo* were available and only 1 or 2 per cent of people with satellite television had ever watched them. Though a number of televangelists in the United States are keen to take their gospel message to unchristian Europe and could solve the problem of European reluctance to give the money needed to buy air time by presenting such work to their home audiences as missionary endeavour, the businessmen who control the satellites know who subscribes and why: working-class families who want live sports for the lads and Hollywood movies for the kids. When NBC bought

Superchannel in 1993, it cancelled all religious programming. One of the major US networks is the Family Channel (it used to be called the Christian Broadcasting Network), which was founded by the Revd Pat Robertson. Robertson built the network on the popularity of his *700 Club* programme, which offers a mix of topical current affairs and evangelical Christian commentary. Not only does Robertson preach for conversions on television but he has even spoken in tongues on the air waves. It is significant that in 1993, when the Family Channel started to be available in Britain on satellite, the *700 Club* was not included in the schedules. As Robertson's son wryly said: 'God is not along for the ride on this one.'

To summarize, that there is an audience for religious programming that is considerably larger than the number of people who are involved in church life is noteworthy, but it tells us more about the historical presence of the churches, about the paternalism of Reith and those who laid the foundations for British broadcasting, and about the nostalgic fondness of the British for hymns than it does about an enduring and meaningful Christianity beyond the churches. By and large religious programmes are most keenly attended to by people who are most religious in the conventional sense; they complement institutional religion rather than offer an alternative expression of an 'implicit' religiosity. Although the recent expansion of the electronic mass media has created the opportunity for a more committed sort of religious broadcasting, the American style of televangelism has as yet had no impact on the secular British and is unlikely to become popular. The United States has televangelism because it has a lot of evangelical Christians, not the other way round.

Legitimating Community Life

As I suggested in the first chapter, a major part of the strength of the Christian church in pre-modern European societies was the way in which it was embedded in the everyday life of the laity. Every significant event (and many minor ones) in the round of community life was legitimated by the Church's blessing. Marriages were conducted in churches, babies were baptized there, an appropriate time after birth the new mother was received back into the community with a ceremony known as 'the churching of women', and, of course, the dead were buried by the church. To what extent do we still call on religious professionals to add their gloss to these vital events?

The churching of women has altogether disappeared, but babies are still baptized. The size of the Church of England means that we can take its baptismal record as a fairly good index of Protestant baptisms in England and, as we see from Table 2.17, there has been a decline, but it is less marked than that for church membership or attendance, which confirms the view that many people whose links with the Church are slight still wish to use its offices to mark such an important social event. None the less, there has been a real decline, from two-thirds of all births to under a third.

Table 2.17 Baptisms in the Church of England, 1902–1993 (%)

Year	% of live births baptized in the Church of England
1902	65
1927	71
1960	55
1970	47
1993	27

Sources: Peter Brierley, *A Century of British Christianity: Historical Statistics 1900–1985 with Projections to 2000* (Research Monograph 14; London: MARC Europe, 1989; Andrew Brown, 'Birth Celebration without Religion Offered', *Independent*, 23 July 1994.

Clergymen may feel annoyed at being asked to provide a social function for unbelievers but, though the statistics are against them, they can still hope that the babies they baptize will grow up into committed Christians. The tension is greater in the case of the profusion of unchurched adults who wish to be married in church, though the issue is resolving itself by ever larger numbers of couples marrying in civil ceremonies at Registry Offices or not marrying at all. At the turn of the century, almost 70 per cent of English couples marrying did so in the established church. By 1990 this had fallen to under a third. In 1971, 40 per cent of marriages in Britain were civil rather than religious and that had increased to 47 per cent by 1991. In early Victorian Scotland almost all marriages were religious ceremonies; for example, in 1876, 98.9 per cent of weddings were solemnized in churches. Over the subsequent century, the proportion gradually declined. In 1941 it was 87 per cent. The post-war period then saw more rapid decline, and by 1970 it was only 71 per cent, and in 1990, 57 per cent.

The Exception of Northern Ireland

The one part of the United Kingdom where religion still matters is Northern Ireland. The enduring political conflict ensures that people place a premium on preserving their ethnic identity, and religion is a central part of that ethnicity. Although many Northern Catholics are happy to remain part of the United Kingdom, they none the less express their political preferences by voting for nationalist parties. Almost all Protestants vote for parties which wish to maintain the Union with Britain. On almost every aspect of government policy and public administration—support for the Royal Ulster Constabulary, support for a segregated school system, support for initiatives to correct religious imbalances in the workplace—the two communities diverge significantly. In residence, Protestants and Catholics are as segregated as blacks and whites were under South Africa's notorious pass laws. Of fifty-one census wards in Belfast, thirty are more than 90 per cent Protestant or Catholic. Only among the professional middle classes is there any degree of residential mixing.

With almost every aspect of life dominated by the religio-ethnic division, it is not surprising that religion remains much more salient in Northern Ireland than in Britain. More than half the people are church members and attendance is similarly above British norms. Of a 1991 sample, 58 per cent in Northern Ireland but only 15 per cent in Britain claimed to attend church frequently and that level of involvement is reflected in the size and status of the clergy. Although the Catholic Church throughout Ireland has recently seen a fall in candidates for ordination, it remains buoyant compared to its sister church in England, and the Irish Presbyterian Church (the largest Protestant church in Northern Ireland) has no difficulty attracting candidates. In 1990 there were 438 ministers; in 1943 there were 570. This represents a shrinking of only 23 per cent; half the fall in the clergy of the Church of Scotland or the Church of England. In addition there are some fifty ministers in the Free Presbyterian Church, which was founded by Ian Paisley in the 1950s. If they were included in the Presbyterian total, the decline would be only 14 per cent.

There has been a marked decline in the number of clergy in the episcopal Church of Ireland: from 1,617 in 1901 to 535 in 1990, but when we separate the figures for Northern Ireland and the Irish Republic, we can see the main reason for that fall. Although it styles itself the Presbyterian Church *in Ireland*, the large majority of Presbyterian congregations were in the six counties that formed Northern Ireland. On the other hand, prior to partition, two-thirds of Church of Ireland congregations were in the twenty-six counties which formed the Irish Free State (later the Irish Republic). In Northern Ireland the episcopal Church retains 77 per cent of its 1926 size, but in the Irish Republic it stands at only 34 per cent of its size at the first census after partition. In England and Scotland the main churches have shrunk despite population growth. In the Irish Republic, the main Protestant church declined rapidly in line with the decline of the Protestant population.

Attitude surveys show that the people of Northern Ireland, both inside and outside the churches, hold considerably more traditional religious views than the rest of the United Kingdom. The differences between images and strength of belief in God are abundantly clear from the two columns in Table 2.10. There are five times as many atheists and agnostics in Britain as in Northern Ireland, the vague 'higher-power' option is not at all popular, and more than half the sample 'know God exists'—a certainty which is managed by under a quarter of the British respondents. There are also very clear differences on specific matters of doctrine. Because it is significant for our wider understanding of religious change, I will spell these out. When people in Britain joke 'We will soon be landing in Belfast. Please put your watch back fifty years', they are expressing an important truth. In the first chapter I argued that the gradual relaxation of the exclusivist claims made by the British churches and sects, their increasing toleration and cooperation, and the psychologization and liberalization of mainstream Christianity were in large part a response to the fragmentation of the religious culture. Being divided into a large number of groups that could not agree, British Christians first agreed to differ, then agreed that their differences did not matter, and finally agreed that there were not, really, any actual differences. But increasing tolerance is not the inevitable response to diversity. Where there are just one or two large fissures and social divisions stack up rather than cut across each other, one may end up with increased toleration within two camps and correspondingly bitter conflict between them.

In the 1920s Presbyterianism in Ulster, like the rest of European Protestantism, was touched by 'modernizing' trends in biblical scholarship and theology and by ecumenical tendencies in church relations, but these did not develop because the conflict between Protestants and Catholics gave such a high premium to orthodoxy and solidarity on both sides. It was impossible to separate religion and politics. The nineteenth-century slogan 'Home Rule is Rome Rule' remained evocative. For liberal Protestants to suggest more friendly relations with the Catholic Church was to be suspected of encouraging Catholic nationalists. Ian Paisley was

able successfully to found a church *and* a party because he could advertise both with the same claim: the establishment was compromising
with the enemy. Paisley's Free Presbyterian Church was founded in
the relative calm of the 1950s and it did not take off until the late
1960s when the start of the present Troubles suddenly gave substance
to Paisley's claim that liberal tendencies in unionist politics and
ecumenical tendencies in the Presbyterian Church were part of the
same process—surrender to Rome—and both were to be firmly
resisted.

An elder of the Church of Scotland in 1890 could walk into very many
Irish Presbyterian or Free Presbyterian congregations now and feel
thoroughly at home. The enduring political conflict in Ulster has
retarded the developments that 'naturally' occurred in Scottish or
English churches. Without being terribly misled, we can look at the differences between religious beliefs of Protestants in Northern Ireland
and Britain as both a contemporary portrait of the two places and as a
picture of how much British Protestantism has changed.

The 1991 British Social Attitudes Survey asked the Northern Ireland
sample if 'you have had a turning-point in your life when you committed yourself to Christ'. It also asked all respondents some very specific
questions about life after death, miracles, the existence of the Devil,
and the like, which allowed me to identify a clear 'evangelical'
Protestant position and a clear 'liberal' sample. It also offered three different ways of describing the Bible: 'the actual word of God . . . to be
taken literally, word for word', 'the inspired word of God, but not everything should be taken literally, word for word', and 'an ancient book of
fables, legends, history and moral teachings recorded by man'. The first
position is that of the biblical literalist; the last that of the modernist.
The proportions of Protestants giving each answer are presented in
Table 2.18.

The first important point to note is that Ulster Protestantism is not
conservative because conservative Protestant sects are better represented (though they are). For every denomination, members in
Northern Ireland are much more likely than their co-religionists in
Britain to have been born again, to be evangelical in theology, and to
take a literalist view of the scriptures. The second salient point is the
scale of difference. Except among the Baptists, who are few, the idea
that the Bible is literally the word of God is almost unheard of in Britain
and common in Northern Ireland, accepted by a third of the members
of the Presbyterian Church, the largest Protestant denomination!

When pushed on the nature of their beliefs, Christians would accept
that, unlike, for example, Judaism, which is the religion of the Jewish

Table 2.18 Protestant Beliefs, Britain and Northern Ireland, 1991 (%)

Affiliation	Conversion				Theology				View of Bible			
	Born again		Not born again		Evangelical		Liberal		Literalist		Modernist	
	GB	NI	GB	NI	GB	NI	GB	NI	GB	NI	GB	NI
Episcopalian	n.a.	19	n.a.	81	1	14	13	12	2	31	18	14
Methodist	n.a.	21	n.a.	79	2	15	4	8	1	25	12	17
Presbyterian	n.a.	28	n.a.	72	2	20	14	8	3	35	19	12
Baptist	n.a.	70	n.a.	30	18	31	—	21	15	45	3	—
Free Presbyterian	n.a.	64	n.a.	36	—	32	—	11	—	37	—	5
Brethren	n.a.	93	n.a.	7	—	81	1	—	—	69	—	—
Other Protestant	n.a.	79	n.a.	21	11	5	1	2	16	39	3	7

Notes: n.a. = not asked.
A dash signifies categories with no occupants or so few that they are rounded up to less than 0.49%.

Source: Steve Bruce and Fiona Alderdice, 'Religious Belief and Behaviour', in Peter Stringer and Gillian Robinson (eds.), Social Attitudes in Northern Ireland: The Third Report, 1992–93 (Belfast: Blackstaff, 1993).

people, their religion has a universal mission. Christianity speaks to all people alike and, while parents may teach their beliefs to their children, salvation is not genetically transmitted. However, this has never prevented particular ethnic groups or nations claiming to be especially blessed nor has it stopped peoples using religious ideas and language to understand their arguments with their neighbours. The fact that the two ethnic groups in Northern Ireland are identified by two distinct and competing religions means that religious leaders will tend to a partial view of their role. Coincidentally each side sees doing God's will as being much the same as 'representing my people'. This is not to say that religious professionals on both sides do not feel an obligation to soften ancient divisions. Rather it is to recognize that the strength of the ethnic 'pull' on the churches is such that the leaders can only follow their people.

The Reach and Consequences of Religion

Thus far this review of religion in the United Kingdom has not directly addressed what might reasonably be regarded as the main question: what difference does religion make? In describing the gradual separation of church and state, the historical introduction implicitly began to answer that question when it talked of the gradual shrinking of the remit of the churches and, by implication, of religion. Although it is a gross simplification, a useful way of describing changes in the social meaning of religion is to say that its 'reach' has been reduced. In most modern societies, even those (such as the United States) where religion remains popular, it no longer has the social importance that it once had. Its influence is largely confined to the private world of the family, the weekend, and leisure activities. It is seen far more as a matter of personal preference than as a divinely ordained necessity.

Does private and voluntary religion have identifiable wider consequences for the lives of those who accept it? That is actually very difficult to answer, except in those cases where a church demands some action of its members that is clearly deviant in the wider society. Outside the small Protestant sects, such challenges to conventional mores are rare. The Exclusive Brethren place such store on maintaining their spiritual purity that they cannot join associations which have non-Brethren members. Their refusal to join trade unions and professional associations means that certain occupations are closed to them. In 1964 the House of Lords refused to pass a bill which would allow

Brethren pharmacists to sit the relevant professional examinations but not join the Pharmaceutical Society. Brethren pharmacists had to choose between job and sect. Some sects will not accept certain medical therapies (such as blood transfusions). Others have a 'conscientious objection' to war. But beyond these small groups, what difference does religion make?

One division between believers and non-believers is that the former are keen to assert that religion does or should matter, not just to themselves but to others. That may sound obvious, but consider responses to a survey item which asked people if 'Right and wrong should be based on God's laws'. The Northern Ireland sample was predictably theocratic. Sixty-three per cent of Catholics, the same proportion of mainstream Protestants, and a full 88 per cent of conservative Protestants agreed that morality was a matter for God. However, in the British sample, if one looks only at the three-quarters of the total sample who identified with a Christian denomination, one finds that as many people were 'neutral' or disagreed as agreed.

One might suppose that a person's religion would tell us something about his or her political preferences. It clearly does where there is an 'ethnic' basis to religious identity. Although the pattern is weakening, Scottish Catholics still have a clear bias to the Labour Party (a residue of the Irish community's distinctive social history) and are only slowly overcoming their distrust of the Scottish National Party, which is still seen by many as a rural Protestant party. The strong links between ethnicity, religion, and politics in Northern Ireland have already been mentioned. But if one considers Britain, the effect of the small number of Catholics disappears and one has a slight association between various indices of religiosity and support for the Conservative rather than the Labour party. In the 1991 British Social Attitudes Survey, support between the three major parties was divided 44 per cent for the Conservatives, 40 per cent for Labour, and 16 per cent for the Liberal Democrats. However, of those who said they prayed more than once a week, 50 per cent identified with the Tories and 36 per cent with Labour. Forty-six per cent of those who thought of themselves as religious preferred the Tories; 39 per cent preferred Labour. Forty-seven per cent of those who frequently went to church identified with the Conservatives; 35 per cent chose Labour. So there is some connection but it is not great and it seems very largely explained by age; older people are more religious and more likely to support the Conservatives.

Using the same source, we can go beyond party labels to look at political attitudes which broadly represent the left–right divide in politics. Should the government give priority to fighting inflation or to keeping unemployment down? Should the government increase taxes and public expenditure? Should there be more or less privatization? Should it be the task of government to reduce income differentials? On none of these questions did church-goers differ significantly from non-church-goers. However, before this is taken as proof that church leaders are out of tune with their members when they criticize Conservative party free-market economics, it should be noted that the most common positions—those from which church-goers were not departing—were not those favoured by the government!

It is possible that the distinctive history of the Catholic community in Britain—only recently emerged from a position of social and economic deprivation—would give it distinctly different views and that liberal church-going Catholics would cancel out conservative church-going Protestants, but examining each group separately produced no stronger relationships, except in one regard. For Catholics, there is a statistically significant relationship between church-going and the position taken on the question of whether the government should give priority to protecting civil rights or cutting crime. Regular mass-goers were keener than the average respondent to see cutting crime as the priority.

Church-goers were no more in favour of stiffer prison sentences than the general public and were slightly more likely than the general public to oppose capital punishment. They were perfectly normal in their attitude to tax evasion and benefit cheating; like everyone else, they were against the first and very much against the second. There was a series of questions about gender roles and working wives and here too the church-goers did not stand out from the rest of the sample.

One aspect of personal behaviour that we expect to be associated with piety is 'temperance' or abstinence from alcohol and tobacco. For the last century evangelical Protestants have made abstinence an article of faith. If you were 'chapel' you did not drink. There has been a strong temperance movement in the Catholic Church but, being a very broad, pan-community church with a strong working-class presence, there has also been a long tradition of Catholics smoking and drinking. The numbers involved are too small to allow very strong patterns to emerge, but one remarkable finding is that, while half of Ulster's conservative Protestants do not drink, only 8 per cent of their British counterparts are abstainers.

The one area where clear differences did emerge was sexuality and related socio-moral issues. Church-goers were more likely than the average respondent to be opposed to sexual intercourse before marriage and to homosexuality, but the association was weak. The one item which produced a strong and statistically significant association was abortion. Compared to the rest of the sample, Catholic and Protestant church-goers were very strongly opposed to abortion.

Social surveys are, of course, not the only source of information about attitudes and I have been at pains to stress the fallibility of these sources. However, the general conclusions fit with my own very clear impressions and with those of others who have closely observed British religious life. Except in the small sects, believers do not possess distinctive attitudes or behave in ways that distinguish them from their colleagues and neighbours. Put crudely, though committed Christians share a distinctive world-view and may well as a result be happier, more content, or more personally fulfilled, they are not behaviourally distinctive.

The Shift to the Right

It is to those small sects, or at least the sectarian end of the religious continuum, that we now turn. Not all trends in British Christianity point downwards. When we talk of the decline of the churches, we should more properly talk of the decline of liberal and mainstream Christianity. Not all the many churches and chapels that have been abandoned by the major denominations have become carpet warehouses. Some have been bought and reopened by small groups of evangelicals, fundamentalists, and pentecostalists. Much of this growth is a result of recruiting Afro-Caribbean migrants (and will be discussed in the next chapter), but leaving them aside we still find a general pattern of resilience to secularization increasing as we move from 'left' to 'right' across the Protestant spectrum. Admittedly from very small bases, a number of sects have shown marked growth. The Church of the Nazarene, which was founded in 1906, has grown from about 1,000 members in 1940 to 5,000 in 1990. In the 1920s there were 360 congregations in the Assemblies of God; there are now over 600. The Elim Pentecostal Church now has about 45,000 members in 473 congregations; in 1939 there were 280 congregations.

Conservative resilience can also be found among the 'new' religions of the late nineteenth century. Though there are around 45,000 Spiritualists in Britain, there were almost twice as many pre-1939. In contrast, the Jehovah's Witnesses and the Mormons (or the Church of Jesus Christ of Latter-day Saints) have grown slowly but steadily and continue to grow. In 1943 there were 11,000 'Publishers' (as Witnesses are known); by 1963 there were 47,000, and there are now some 116,000. There are now almost 150,000 Mormons in Britain.

Within broad Protestant traditions, the most conservative elements have generally survived the last three decades in the best shape. The United Reformed Church (URC) was formed in 1972 from the merger of the Presbyterian Church of England and the majority of congregations in the Congregational Union of England and Wales. The URC has shown a faster rate of decline than did any of its components before the merger. The Congregationalists who stayed out, largely because they were more evangelical than they expected the new body to be, have retained roughly the number of congregations and members they had in 1972. The URC has lost half of the members it had at the merger.

A similar point can be made about Scottish Presbyterianism. Between 1975 and 1992, the liberal United Free Church lost 45 per cent of its members and the mainstream Church of Scotland lost 28 per cent, but the conservative Free Church lost only 10 per cent and the very small and very conservative Free Presbyterian Church (not to be confused with Ian Paisley's body of the same name) has remained about even.

The most eye-catching example of the same trend has been the growth of the independent 'house church' or Restoration movement. Mostly formed in the early 1970s, many 'house churches' have now grown to be sizeable congregations with their own premises. The movement is structured around a number of loose associations, usually linked to a powerful preacher, and involving subscribing to certain magazines, buying cassettes of the preacher's sermons, and attending annual conventions such as the Dales Bible Week. That these groups are not organized into national organizations means that figures for their size can only be guesses, but one reasonable estimate supposes that the House Church Movement has grown from some 44,000 members in 1979 to 109,000 in 1989. The groups were newsworthy, of course, because they were growing, but they also stood out by going so much against the secularizing tide. They were evangelical in doctrine, pentecostal or 'charismatic' in speaking in tongues, healing and prophesying, and distinctly authoritarian. Where the leaders of the mainstream churches have trouble in extracting any form of obedience from even their committed members, the 'Shepherds' of the house churches are looked to for guidance on even such mundane questions as changes of job or residence and such personal matters as the suitability of marriage partners. One respect in which they differed from the older pentecostal churches was in the enthusiastic and emotional style of their services, which owed much to the liveliness and informality of Afro-Caribbean and white American styles. They also differed in attracting significant numbers of well-educated professional people.

If we accept the general conclusion that the decline of mainstream

Christianity has been accompanied by resilience and even growth on the right, how do we explain the trend? One possibility, which has been developed in a number of sophisticated theories about human spirituality, is that people have needs which can be met only by supernatural beliefs. It may be that our desires so persistently outstrip our circumstances that, no matter how much life improves, we always feel relatively deprived and are thus in the market for the promise that the afterlife will be better than this one. It may be that, no matter how much our knowledge of the material world improves, we can always have 'ultimate' questions about the nature and purpose of human existence which cause us to seek answers beyond the natural world. If these and other formulations of similar ideas have merit, then those liberal churchmen who argued that the supernatural elements should be removed from religious beliefs so as to make them more palatable to modern people made a big mistake.

However, this line of reasoning runs into a slight problem with the evidence. If it were the case that the resilience of conservative Protestantism is explained by it better serving our needs, then it should be the case that people defect from the unsatisfactory liberal churches to more conservative ones, but this is not what has happened. As we know from detailed studies of membership rolls, the main reason for leaving the Church of England and the Church of Scotland is death, not displeasure. It is their failure to compensate for the mortality of existing members by recruiting their offspring which explains why these denominations have declined. On the other side, very little of the growth of conservative churches can be explained by them attracting either disappointed long-term members of liberal and mainstream churches or frustrated atheists. Rather they have sustained themselves primarily from recruiting and holding their own offspring, and this is true even for sects such as Jehovah's Witnesses and the Mormons which put considerable effort into door-to-door recruitment of new members. Even new bodies, such as the independent evangelical and charismatic congregations, have grown largely by attracting young adults from other sects and from the evangelical wings of the major denominations.

This suggests that the decline of the mainstream and the resilience of the conservative options should be treated as distinct rather than related phenomena and each explained in terms of its own internal dynamics. And those can be very simply summarized. Sects, with their insistence that they and they alone possess the saving truth, encourage their adherents to work hard at maintaining their faith and transmitting it to the children. They will organize their social world so as to reduce contact with unbelievers and strengthen the social bonds that maintain the community of the Godly. They will still lose potential members, but they will retain enough to grow slightly. The denominational form, because it concedes that its virtues can be found not only in other religions but even in secular beliefs and actions, removes the incentives to socialize the next generation and to create an ideological ghetto. Being so little set aside from the world, it offers little to the unchurched, though it will always recruit some children of sectarians who will be attracted by the possibility of retaining some of their old faith but losing the dogmatism and petty restrictions of the sect. This suggests the following pattern of migration. Sects are the greenhouse of faith. Some members are retained, and some are lost to denominations and some to the secular world. Denominations lose members by death, and recruit almost no atheists, and only small numbers of sectarians.

Summary

What can we conclude about Christianity in modern Britain? Most obviously, in size, popularity, and influence, the mainstream Christian denominations have declined markedly. Small conservative Protestant sects have shown more resilience and there has been some growth in conservative Protestantism, but the numbers involved do nothing to compensate for the collapse of the main churches. However impressive the growth of the independent evangelical sector, it barely dents the mass of the unchurched. Most British people now have no church connection and are linked to organized religion only by their infrequent attendance at *rites of passage*, by their residual respect for 'religion' (which they think is a good thing), and by their nostalgic fondness for church buildings and hymns.

There are enormous difficulties conceptualizing, let along measuring, 'folk' or 'implicit' or 'common' (as contrasted with institutional) religion. It will always be possible to argue that departure from the churches represents only a lack of willingness to participate in voluntary associations and not a general loss of faith in the supernatural products which people once consumed in those voluntary associations. Given the problems of knowing what is going on in people's heads, it will always be extremely difficult, if not impossible, to produce evidence which resolves the issue finally. However, the data provided here offer little reason to suppose that beyond the churches there is any enduring self-standing 'implicit' religiosity. Against those who would see implicit religion as some sort of compensation for the decline of *explicit* religion, I would suggest that the former be seen as an echo of the latter and not as an alternative. As formal religion has declined so has the specific detail and salience of religious images, thinking, and behaviour outside the churches. The Christian churches have lost their ability to shape popular thinking. In so far as many people in Britain continue to think that there is more to the world than meets the eye, their images of the supernatural are no longer structured by Christian precepts. They are amorphous and idiosyncratic and have few, if any, behavioural consequences.

Further Reading

A vast amount of statistical material has been presented in compressed form in this chapter. Figures for congregations, clergy, and church members have been drawn from Leslie Paul, *The Deployment and Payment of the Clergy* (London: Church Information Office, 1966); Robert Currie, Alan D. Gilbert, and Lee Horsley, *Churches and Churchgoers: Patterns of Church Growth in the British Isles since 1700* (Oxford: Oxford University Press, 1977); and *A Christian Yearbook 1943 Edition* (London: SCM Press, 1943).

An invaluable resource is the enormous body of research material produced by Peter Brierley of MARC Europe (later the Christian Research Association) and his various collaborators. In 1977 and 1978 he produced the *UK Protestant Missions Handbook*. This evolved into the *UK Christian Handbook*, which has now appeared in nine editions (from 1980 to 1994). Brierley's *A Century of British Christianity: Historical Statistics 1900–1985 with Projections to 2000* (Research Monograph 14; MARC Europe, 1985) summarizes a vast body of statistics.

Brierley undertook a number of clergy-based censuses of church attendance and the data are available as *Prospects for the Eighties: From a Census of the Churches in 1979* (London: Bible Society, 1980); *Prospects for Wales: From a Census of the Churches in 1982* (London: Bible Society/MARC Europe, 1983); *Prospects for Scotland: From a Census of the Churches in 1984* (Edinburgh: The Bible Society of Scotland, 1985); and *Prospects for the Nineties: Trends and Tables from the English Church Census* (London: MARC Europe, 1991). The results of the 1989 English Church Census are summarized in Brierley, *'Christian' England: What the English Church Census Reveals* (London: MARC Europe, 1991). The more recent studies and a large number of important research monographs are available from the Christian

Research Association, 4 Footscray Road, Eltham, London SE11 4BT.

The data on religious beliefs and attitudes come from the following sources. Most of the pre-1987 information is taken from regular surveys conducted by the Gallup Organization: see George H. Gallup (ed.), *The Gallup International Public Opinion Polls: Great Britain 1937–1975* (New York: Random House, 1976). The 1981 data come from the work of the European Values Study Group; see David Gerard, 'Religious Attitudes and Values', in Mark Abrams, David Gerard, and Noel Timms, *Values and Social Change in Britain* (London: Macmillan, 1985), 50–92, and David Barker, Loek Halman, and Astrid Vloet (eds.), *The European Values Study 1981–1990: Summary Report* (London: Gordon Cook Foundation/European Values Group, 1992). The 1991 results come from my original analysis of the data in the British Social Attitudes Survey of that year, which added a lengthy supplement of questions on religion to its annually repeated questions. The data for the run of surveys from 1983 to 1992 are available from the Economic and Social Research Council Data Archive at the University of Essex and are reported in the following: Social and Community Planning Research, *British Social Attitudes Cumulative Sourcebook: The First Six Years* (Aldershot: Gower, 1991); Roger Jowell, Lindsay Brook, Gillian Prior, and B. Taylor (eds.), *British Social Attitudes: The 9th Report* (Aldershot: Dartmouth, 1992); Peter Stringer and Gillian Robinson (eds.), *Social Attitudes in Northern Ireland, 1990–91 Edition* (Belfast: Blackstaff, 1991), *Social Attitudes in Northern Ireland: The Second Report, 1991–92* (Belfast: Blackstaff, 1992), and *Social Attitudes in Northern Ireland: The Third Report, 1992–93* (Belfast: Blackstaff, 1993). International comparisons of the BSA data can be found in Roger Jowell, Lindsay Brook, and Lizanne Dowds (eds.), *International Social Attitudes: The 10th BSA Report* (Aldershot: Dartmouth, 1993).

General data on religious beliefs and behaviour, as well as specific information on attitudes to religious broadcasting, are taken from a series of studies by the Independent Broadcasting Authority (IBA), later the Independent Television Commission (ITC): IBA, *Lonely People and the Media* (London: IBA, 1978); Michael Svennevig, Ian Haldane, Sharon Speirs, and Barrie Gunter, *Godwatching: Viewers, Religion and Television* (London: John Libbey/IBA, 1989); and Barrie Gunter and Rachel Vinney, *Seeing is Believing: Religion and Television in the 1990s* (London: John Libbey/ITC, 1994).

For an introductory discussion of implicit religion, see Edward Bailey, 'The Implicit Religion of Contemporary Society: An Orientation and a Plea for its Study', *Religion*, 13 (1983), 69–83.

Chapter Three

Multi-Cultural Britain

Britain has seen very little inward migration in the modern period and hence changes in its religious culture have mostly been the result of the evolution and fragmentation of a single tradition. In this chapter I want to look at the immigrant religions of Britain, both because they are interesting in their own right and because they raise important issues about the place of religion in our public life.

The Jews

Since the Middle Ages there has been a Jewish community in Britain and it has periodically been topped up with the arrival of Jews escaping persecution in other parts of Europe and in Muslim lands. In 1800 there were probably 30,000 Jews in England. By 1881 the number had doubled. Between then and 1905 somewhere in the region of 100,000 Russian Jews settled in Britain. A large proportion of these poor Yiddish-speaking migrants congregated in Whitechapel and Spital-fields, where, as happened with the Irish earlier, they were often blamed by native Londoners for the manifest social ills of the East End.

That Jews moved to, rather than from, Britain shows that, in the context of European anti-Semitism, Britain was relatively liberal. Jews had benefited both from general legislation aimed at removing civil disabilities from Protestant dissenters and from reforms specifically directed at the position of Jews, but there remained considerable anti-Jewish sentiment, not only among the urban poor who resented any migrant group which threatened to worsen their already dreadful conditions but also in the English ruling classes. As recent biographies of Winston Churchill demonstrate, it was commonplace for the English ruling classes to despise 'yids', and the 1920s novels of Dornford Yates were unremarkable for their time in frequently using Jewish characters, either as stock villains or as glaring examples of the lack of breeding and manners among the *nouveau riche*. While more noble reasons were offered at the time, Britain's unwillingness to publicize the plight of European Jews in the Nazi holocaust reflected continued anti-Semitism, but the last fifty years have seen that sentiment dissolve as religious identification has weakened, Jews have become well integrated, and more readily identifiable minorities have arrived to take the brunt of racist feeling.

As with other minorities to be discussed in this section, it is a mistake to regard all Jews as much of a muchness. The community has always been internally divided first by ethnic origin and then, as each wave became Anglicized, by the religious issues of how the faith should be lived out in a modern secular society.

Unlike the case in many Eastern European countries, nineteenth-century British Jews were not compelled by law to form 'ghettos' (the word is Yiddish in origin), but the commonplace pressures of being a migrant minority in an often hostile land gave Jews one good reason to cluster, and the religious requirement to maintain a distinctive way of life added another. Almost a third of Britain's Jewish population of around 300,000 people is to be found in north-west London. The decline in numbers which has resulted from marriage out of the community and gradual assimilation has accelerated the trend to concentration. In the nineteenth century there was a thriving Jewish community involved in Belfast's linen industry. The Troubles persuaded many Jews to move and by the 1970s the community was too small to support a rabbi or a kosher butcher. As children grew up and left home, elderly relatives took the opportunity to move to Liverpool, Manchester, or London. There are now only 400 Jews in Northern Ireland. From a much higher base line—50,000 in 1957—the Jewish community in Glasgow has also shrunk to less than a fifth of that size. But even in its strong centres, Judaism is under threat. The 1990s community—with 320 synagogues—is only two-thirds what it was in the 1950s. The number of synagogue marriages has fallen from around 1,500 a year in the late 1970s to fewer than 1,000 in 1994. Part of that decline is actually a victory. Thousands of British Jews have migrated to Israel. But a third of Jews are marrying 'out' and the home is such an important centre for Jewish ritual and observance that such intermarriage now jeopardizes the future of the faith, which is why the Jewish Marriage Council set up Connect, an introduction agency to which young Jews anonymously submit biographical details for circulation in a bulletin. In 1994 a new charity Jewish Continuity was established with the remit of 'intensifying ethnicity'.[1] In one sense, British Jews face the

WHAT JEWS BELIEVE

- Judaism is a monotheistic religion. It has one God, who judges human actions and rewards and punishes as appropriate.

- God's will is known through the divinely inspired *Torah* or teaching, contained in Genesis, Exodus, Leviticus, Numbers, and Deuteronomy and elaborated in the rest of the Old Testament. This canon is accompanied by the *Talmud*, a written compilation of once-oral traditions of textual exposition and interpretation.

- God's laws determine Jewish norms and penetrate every facet of the life of the individual and the community. The religious leader of the Jews is not the priest skilled in sacramental ritual but the *rabbi*, skilled in interpreting the *Torah* and accompanying commentaries to discern how God's laws should be applied to particular situations and problems. Being a Jew is much more a matter of correct behaviour than of belief, or orthopraxy rather than orthodoxy. Prominent in giving the public face to Judaism are the complex dietary regulations derived from the book of Leviticus.

- Prayers, family and congregational, are central to Jewish life, as are keeping the Sabbath holy, and observing the major festivals which mark symbolically important experiences in the early history of the Jews.

- Although Jews accept the possibility of conversion, they do not seek converts. Jews are born Jewish. As an elderly Israeli rabbi who had arrived to spend a year leading the Belfast community said in response to a journalist who asked if he planned to convert the Christians to Judaism: 'I will be happy to convert the Jews to Judaism!'

- Jews believe that a Messiah will come to redeem his people and to establish the kingdom of God on earth but, as in Christianity, most Jews do not expect this to happen soon and are not consciously oriented to this *Adventist* option. However, some groups of the *Lubavitch* sect of Orthodox Jews do expect the imminent end of the prevailing order and were greatly disappointed by the death in 1994 of the *rebbe* (or spiritual leader) they took to be the Messiah.

same problem as conservative Protestants or Catholics. Does the community turn inward and try to create the social and cultural institutions that will allow it to regain the hegemony of the 'church' form of religion? Or does it embrace diversity, allow its distinctiveness to be eroded, and reconceptualize itself as a 'denomination'? With some exaggeration, that choice is the division between Orthodox Jews and the Reform and Liberal traditions (to which about 20 per cent of British synagogues adhere). The particular problem for Jews is that, because

Judaism is inherited rather than acquired, they cannot either try to replace defectors with converts or, as liberal Christians can, find much comfort in supposing that, though their particular religion is disappearing, its ethos will none the less pervade and improve society at large. The ghetto-building route is that favoured by the *Chasidim*, who have recently pioneered Jewish housing schemes. The Agudas Israel Housing Association in 1994 completed a development of houses and flats in Stoke Newington, north London, which are specially designed to make conformity with Jewish laws easier. They have timers on the lighting circuits and automatic lifts so that residents can live in comfort without breaking the rules against working on the Sabbath. So that orthodox Jews can easily meet the requirement to remember the forty years in the wilderness by living 'in the open' for eight days each year, the living-rooms have removable rooflights.

It may well be that such imaginative reconciling of traditional demands and modern circumstances has come too late. Though British Jews are more religiously observant than the general population, the levels of commitment may already be too low for the community to reproduce itself despite its concentration in ever narrower areas. In a 1992 survey a third of Jews said they went to synagogue once a week and 21 per cent went once a month but almost half went only once a year.

The New Commonwealth Immigrants

Although its importance as a cultural marker was not appreciated at the time, a significant event in British social history occurred in 1948, when a former German pleasure cruiser, the *Empire Windrush*, brought 492 West Indians to work in England. During the 1950s there was an average annual inflow of around 10,000 people from the Commonwealth, attracted by the job opportunities offered by the post-war expansion of the economy. Although economic decline slowed this down in the late 1950s, the first arrivals created networks which made possible a rapid rise in migration in the early 1960s. This created pressure for controls, which ironically *increased* the rate as people tried to get in before the barriers came down. The 1962 Act effectively stemmed new migration but allowed those people already resident here to be joined by relatives and dependants.

We can estimate the size of the Afro-Caribbean population of England as being around 600,000. Of these, 17 per cent or one in six were in a Christian church on the day of Brierley's 1989 English Church

Census. That attendance level already marks British West Indians off from the general population, but more striking is the age profile. In contrast to the skewing of most British churches to the elderly and the female, the Black churches had a normal age distribution and a greater proportion of male attenders.

There are Black-led Christian churches which are not pentecostal. The African Methodist Episcopal Church and the African Methodist Episcopal Zion Church were originally formed by Black Methodists in the United States unhappy at the racism of their denominations. However, the overwhelming majority—perhaps 80 per cent—of British Afro-Carribeans who are in Christian churches are to be found in independent pentecostal churches and it is their religion which will be described here.

WHAT PENTECOSTALISTS BELIEVE

- Pentecostalists are theologically conservative evangelical Protestants. They accept the Apostles' Creed (see p. 15) and they share the evangelical stress on the need for a personal-conversion experience.

- Pentecostalists, like the early Methodists, are more concerned with religious experience than with dogma and doctrine. Lively singing and extemporized prayer are more important in their worship than the exposition of doctrine.

- Pentecostalists differ from other conservative Protestants in believing that the gifts of the Holy Spirit given to the Apostles (the powers of prophecy, healing, and speaking in 'the tongues of men and angels') were not time-bound but are still available to the true Christian.

- For the evangelical, holiness is attained by conversion and by water baptism (with some evangelicals insisting that the baptism be by full immersion). To these the pentecostalist adds a further 'work of grace': the baptism in the Holy Spirit. This is often an ecstatic experience signalled by acquiring the ability to speak in tongues.

- Black Pentecostalism differs from that of the predominantly white Assemblies of God and the Elim Pentecostal Church in incorporating some of the content (the stress on healing, for example) and much of the style (the call-and-response style of singing, the dancing) of the Caribbean folk religions which preceded and continued to flourish alongside Protestantism in the West Indies.

In the 1950s Blacks found most white congregations extremely uninviting. In some they were deliberately snubbed and in others ignored but, even without racism and prejudice, they would have found most English congregations uncongenial. Most migrants were young adults; in most white congregations the elderly were in the majority. 'Most white congregations also lacked characteristics which black Christians considered concomitants of authentic faith and spirituality: demonstrable love, life and spiritual power; a high degree of visible Christian commitment; a strong sense of community and full opportunity to participate at every level.'[2]

Pryce's *Endless Pressure* offers an excellent description of the world of black Pentecostalists in Bristol. Pryce describes the church as a 'religion of the oppressed' in the sense that 'the Saints', as he calls them, are reinterpreting Christianity to suit their position as working-class Blacks in a white society. As he puts it: 'If one cannot accept society or be aggressive towards it with a view to reforming it, then one can devalue the significance of this world by withdrawing from it in a community of like-minded individuals and projecting one's hopes into a supernatural and otherworldly Kingdom.'[3] Part of the appeal is to be welcomed among friends. In that sense the closed world of the Saints is a form of cultural defence, a way of replacing the unflattering status hierarchies of the outside world with ones which do not devalue and denigrate Blacks. But it is also clear that, whether or not they intend to do this, the Saints are also providing themselves and their children with a set of values appropriate to the new world in which they find themselves; that is, their religion assists them in making the transition from the old to the new. The inward-looking community not only provides a place where the Saints can feel good about themselves but also provides them with the character and values that will allow them to do well in the wider society. Saints believe that God's grace and spirit cannot enter an unclean body. Hence they do not drink alcohol and they do not smoke. Swearing, dancing, and mixing with sinners are also prohibited, as is flashy dressing; hence male Saints wear dark suits, white shirts and ties. Sexual relations are only permitted within a traditional marriage. As one preacher said:

And one more thing before I stop. You don't go around giving your bodies to immorality either. Sexual relations outside marriage is an abominable and horrifying sin! Our bodies are the receptacles of the Holy Ghost and they are not to be pampered and petted, kissed and rubbed and inflamed in the erotic regions, to the point where you are afraid to stand up![4]

Puritanism prevents the Saints falling into the behaviour patterns that make it so difficult for the poor to stop being poor. The sanctity of the family is vital. Rich people can afford the break-up of the home, but being a single parent (and usually that means a mother) is one of the major causes of poverty and for those already near the bottom the collapse of the family is often enough to push them below the ice. Drinking, drug-taking, and sexual promiscuity are doubly costly; they are themselves expensive and they often lead to the loss of reputation and, with it, the loss of a chance of retaining a well-paying job.

As well as prohibiting the dangerous, Pentecostalism also encourages the positive. Like the Boy Scouts, the Saints are instructed and encouraged to develop and maintain a very positive character and a cheery disposition. A Saint does not get depressed or angry, is trustworthy and diligent, and combines personal autonomy and self-reliance with a willingness to play a very active and supportive part in the community of Saints. That community is itself important, not just because it controls deviance but also because it provides members with the positive benefit of mutual support.

In short, like the radical Protestant sects of the eighteenth and nineteenth centuries, Pentecostalism not only reconciles a subordinate people to their position but offers an ethical code and a model character which offer some hope of improving that position and a supportive environment in which to face the trials of everyday life. That is, Pentecostalism is highly adaptive.

Muslims

The United Kingdom's ten-yearly population census asks people to choose an ethnic identity. Although some of the categories are too broad to tell us much, the summary of the 1991 data presented in Table 3.1 shows the considerable presence of people from South Asia. The majority of Pakistanis and Bangladeshis are Muslims, and various estimates put the size of that community between 900,000 and 1.3 million. Of course, this figure differs from the way we describe Protestant Christian churches in that it counts all members of notionally Muslim families, irrespective of how personally committed they are to their traditional religion.

Another way of dealing with the same data is to ask what is the country of origin of British Muslims. The largest number are Pakistani (357,000). The second largest group is from a variety of Arab countries (121,000) and the third comes from East Africa (99,000). Next in order come India (84,000) and Bangladesh (64,000), and there are roughly equal numbers (50,000) from Iran and from the Turkish part of Cyprus. Because the ability and motivation to migrate declines with the years,

Table 3.1 Ethnic Groups, Britain, 1991 (000s)

Ethnic group	England	Scotland	Wales	Britain
White	44,146	4,933	2,794	51,874
Black Caribbean	487	—	3	500
Black African	206	4	3	212
Black other	170	4	4	178
Indian	824	10	6	840
Pakistani	449	22	6	477
Bangladeshi	159	1	4	163
Chinese	142	10	5	157
Others: Asian	190	5	4	198
Others: non-Asian	272	10	7	290

Source: Peter Brierley and Val Hiscock, UK Christian Handbook: 1994/95 Edition (London: Christian Research Association, 1993); Office of Population Censuses and Surveys, 1991 Census County Monitors (London: HMSO, 1992).

immigrants are usually young people. In 1961 half the Pakistanis were in the young adult range of 25–44, compared with a quarter of the British population as a whole. That age profile, the restrictions on new migration, and a high birth-rate mean that most British Muslims were born in Britain.

The very different backgrounds from which they were drawn and the variety of reasons that caused them to move make it difficult to talk of British Muslims as though they are all alike. The Muslims who came from Gujarat in India tended to be from well-educated professional and trading families, as did the Muslims driven out of East Africa by Kenya's and Uganda's policy of replacing foreigners by native Africans. The more recently arrived Iranians and Arabs tend to be well educated and wealthy, whereas many of the migrants from Pakistan and Bangladesh are poor farmers.

Muslim settlement in Britain is highly concentrated. The 1991 Northern Ireland census, which rather quaintly calls them 'Mohamedans', lists only 972. There are few in Wales and more in Scotland, but the bulk of Muslims are to be found in a small number of parts of England.

Almost half the Muslims in Britain live in and around London. The West Midlands, Yorkshire and the region around Manchester account for two-thirds of the rest. Within the West Midlands, three-quarters of the Pakistani and Bangladeshi community live in Birmingham . . . three-quarters . . . concentrated in just eight of the city's forty-two wards.[5]

WHAT MUSLIMS BELIEVE

- 'Islam' means 'submission to God'. Muslims regards Islam as God's final revelation to mankind, which supersedes the two previous and imperfect versions given to the Jews and the Christians. The prophet Muhammad of the early seventh century AD was the channel for this revelation, which was given to him in the form of the Qur'ān (or Koran).

- The five basic institutions of Islamic law (or *Shari'ah*) incumbent on every male are (1) profession of faith that there is no god except God and Muhammad is his messenger; (2) saying of prayers five times a day; (3) giving of alms (supposedly 2.5 per cent of annual wealth); (4) pilgrimage to Mecca; and (5) observing *Ramadan* with a month of fasting and spiritual disciplines. To these some add the promoting of Islam by a variety of means which may include holy war or *jihad*.

- Muslims are divided into *Sunnis* (the majority) and *Shi'as*. The *Shi'as* add to the above requirements the recognition of the Imam. They hold that God designated a line of immaculate members of the family of 'Ali (the son-in-law and cousin of the Prophet) as charismatic leaders. Since the disappearance of the Twelfth Imam in the ninth century, the line has been hidden, but, like the Messiahs of Judaism and Christianity, the Imam will return to establish a reign of justice and righteousness on the earth.

- Islam, like Judaism, insists that the religious law is all-encompassing. Its primary leaders are not sacramental priests but experts in the exposition of the Qur'ān and the subsequent interpretations of its principles and their application to everyday life. Dietary requirements—meat must be ritually slaughtered and alcohol is forbidden—and dress codes are conspicuous marks of Islam.

- Almost all male Muslims attend congregational prayers on a Friday. Attendance is optional for women and the few who attend pray in a separate room. Mosques conduct business in a variety of languages, according to the ethnicity of the congregation, but the prayers are always said in Arabic, the language of the Qur'ān.

Although there is no precise parallel with Christian denominations and sects, Muslims are divided into a variety of traditions defined by political and ethnic as well as religious divisions. Most British Muslims are *Sunnis*; perhaps 10 per cent are *Shi'as*. British *Sunni* Muslims are further divided into three main groups. The *Barelwi* tend to a popular, superstitious, and worship-oriented mode of Islam which gives high place to saints. If they are the Roman Catholics of Islam, the *Deoband* come close to a Protestant sect, stressing scholarship and asceticism, as do the adherents of *Tablighi Jamaat*. Closely related are the *Ahl-e-hadith*, who accept as authoritative only the Qur'ān and the earliest teachings of *Hadith* (the oral traditions about the life of the Prophet). The third group—*Jamat-i-Islami*—is defined both by a puritanical world-view and by national politics, in that it is an aggressively Islamic party based in Pakistan.

The *Shi'as* are also divided into a number of competing streams defined by which of the line of Imams they accord pride of place. The majority 'Twelvers' hold that the Twelfth Imam (last seen in AD 873) was the *Mahdi* or 'guided one' and is still alive, though hidden, waiting for God's instruction to appear and establish the kingdom of God on earth. 'Seveners' accept the first six Imams but thereafter claim the primacy of Ismail, the elder son of the sixth Imam. An internationally influential section of Seveners is the Nizaris, who believe that the Aga Khan (better known in the West for his wealth and racehorses) is their living Imam.

In both *Sunni* and *Shi'a* traditions, there are groups which hold to a mystical form of Islam known as Sufism. Sufis emphasize the inner spiritual knowledge of God and advocate such disciplines as meditation and ritual dancing as ways of attaining that knowledge. Because it places less store by outward conformity to the requirements of the religious law, Sufism was the strand of Islam which attracted most interest from the cultural samplers of the 1960s hippie era.

How important are the internal divisions of Islam depends on the issue. One cannot imagine a committed Baptist attending Catholic mass if there is no convenient Baptist church, but *Shi'as* will attend a *Sunni* mosque for Friday prayers (though the compliment is not returned). That the Qur'ān and the prayers are in Arabic gives Islam the international unity that Christendom enjoyed when Latin was the language of the universal Christian church. However, despite the formation of a number of local associations of mosques, the divisions do inhibit the development of a nation-wide organization to represent Muslim interests.

The growth of a shared sense of identity as British Muslims is further inhibited by the retention of family ties to the country of origin. Most Muslims from the Indian subcontinent still regard residence in Britain as temporary and families remain close to their home village. Children are sent home for long periods to ensure immersion in the traditional culture. In contrast, the East Africa Asians, who are already one migration and a century away from their land of origin, very obviously have nowhere else to go.

Given that Islam is as broad, as widely distributed, and almost as old

as Christianity, it should be no surprise that there is a looseness of artic-
ulation between styles of Islam and the lives of Muslims who follow
those styles in very different settings. The same set of beliefs can be
interpreted to very different ends in radically different circumstances.
For example, the recent notoriety of Islamic fundamentalism in Iran
has led most Westerners to associate Shi'ites with political radicalism,
but the British reality is very different. Most British Shi'ites are Ismailis
and most are professional people, well integrated into the surrounding
society. What is clear from the increasing literature on Muslims in
Britain is that degrees of distinctiveness are not just, and sometimes not
even, a matter of religion in the narrow sense. Partly they have to do
with the history of the religion. One reason *Shi'as* integrate more readily than *Sunnis* is that for most of their history, and in almost every setting, they have been a minority within Islam. They are used to not
getting their way. Mostly though, and this is true of all migrant religions,
distinctiveness is a matter of the wider culture from which they come;
the life-styles of Gujarati farmers are not those of urban and urbane
East African doctors.

We should also remember that integration is always a matter of interaction between newcomer and host. A minority population may
remain outside the mainstream, not because it wishes to be distinctive,
but because the mainstream will not accept it. This point will be pursued below.

Hindus

A widely used estimate puts the British Hindu population at about
400,000. As with the East African Muslims, many Hindus arrived here in
two steps, having first migrated from Gujarat to Kenya, Tanzania, and
Uganda and then moved here in response to the Africanization of those
countries. According to Knott, about 70 per cent of the Hindu population are Gujarati, 15 per cent come from the Punjab, and the rest come
from such other parts of India as Uttar Pradesh, Bengal, and the south-
ern states. Each ethnic group uses its own language among itself but
uses English or Hindi to talk to Hindus of other ethnic groups.

Hindus are not required to attend a place of communal worship and
much of their religion is done at home. In 1963 Desai could say that
Hindus in Britain do not have temples; there are now about 130 and
they are well attended. Many contain consecrated shrines to Radha and
Krishna or Rama, Sita, and Lakshmī. Although not essential for the reli-

WHAT HINDUS BELIEVE

- The term 'Hindu' simply means 'of India'. As one would expect, given the size of the Indian subcontinent and the ethnic and linguistic diversity of those who have inhabited it, Hinduism is extraordinarily complex and encompasses almost every possible sort of religious belief and practice, from pagan superstition to ascetic and scholarly traditions.

- The heart of the philosophical Hinduism of the Brahmans is *dharma*, which, at the cosmic level, means 'self-subsistence', that which has no antecedent cause, and is comparable to the Christian 'Word'. As it says at the start of John's gospel: 'In the beginning was the Word, and the Word was with God and the Word was God.' It also means 'universal law' or norm, which applies at the moral, the ritual, and the social levels. Every individual has a *dharma* specific to his social status and stage of life. There is also a *dharma* specific to each caste.

- As in Buddhism, the individual's spirit (or *atman*) is thought to be 'really' just an embodiment of the universal soul but, in so far as it has an identity, it is retained through a series of reincarnations.

- Underlying reincarnation and everything else is *karma*, which means both action and the consequences of actions. Rebirth is a profoundly moral process in that the accumulation of good *karma* will ensure a better birth next time round. This doctrine is, not surprisingly, favoured by high-caste Brahmans because it explains their privileges as being deserved by their good actions in previous lives and it reconciles the lower orders to their humble position.

- The good Hindu life has four ends. In addition to *dharma*, there is *artha* (correct behaviour in the material world of productive and economic activity) and *kama* (the pursuit of love and pleasure). Proper action in these spheres will lead to the fourth end: *moksha* or release from the cycle of rebirth. As in the Buddhist tradition, the culmination of religious activity is final departure from the material world.

- There is no single work or canon which contains the authoritative version of divine revelation. Instead of a Pentateuch, the Bible, or the Qur'ān, there are a very large number of sources. The *Vedas*, the oldest of which date back to 3000 BC, contain hymns, ritual instructions, and philosophical observations. Then there are the two great epics: the *Ramayana* and the *Mahabarata*. The latter tells the story of a great battle in which Prince Arjuna is taught the significance of *dharma* by the God Krishna, who acts as his charioteer. The convoluted story shows the dreadful consequences which result when people follow their own interpretation of duty rather than that laid down by Krishna and teaches that the highest morality lies in doing what has to be done, entirely detached from the and teaches that the highest morality lies in doing what has to be done, entirely detached from the consequences. The Hindu text best known in the West, the *Bhagavad-Gita*, is an excerpt from the *Mahabarata* and illustrates the connection between *dharma* and *karma*. There are also a large number of texts which are grouped by the realm of life to which they refer. Thus there is the *Dharma-sutra*, the *Artha-sutra*, and the *Kama-sutra*, the latter well known to salacious Westerners as a sex manual.

- Brahmanic Hinduism is complemented by a theistic devotional strand which worships, among many others, Indra (God of Rain), Surya (Sun), Chadra (Moon), Ganesha (the remover of obstacles, depicted as a creature with four arms and an elephant's head), Yama (death), Sarasvati (Goddess of learning and wife of Brahma), and Lakshmī (Goddess of wealth and wife of Vishnu).

- The philosophical strand readily encompasses the theistic cults by supposing that the variety of deities are 'really' illusory embodiments of the single spirit of cosmic consciousness. They provide a useful channel for the religious consciousness of the less sophisticated, in the same way that the cult of Mary provides a way to God for the less sophisticated Catholic.

gion, temples are still important community centres and very many Hindus attend the temple for major annual festivals such as *Divali*. Smaller numbers attend the temple for regular worship events such as *Puja* and *Arti* (services in which Hindu gods are offered hospitality). The temple is also important as a centre for mother-tongue language teaching and as the place to mark important social events.

Like most Muslim communities, Hindus are divided by ethnic background and by preferences within the common religious tradition but Hindus are further divided by *caste*. Traditionally Hindu society was hierarchically structured into four broad bands which were ordered according to prestige: *Brahmans* formed the intelligentsia and priesthood, *Kshatriyas* the administrative and military caste, *Vaishyas* the merchants and agriculturalists, and *Sudras* the manual labourers. Within the four bands are innumerable more specific occupational groups, called *jati*. Outside these four are the 'untouchables'. Unlike our notion of 'class', caste membership is hereditary. In all the major religious traditions there is an association with class. Particular social circumstances will lead those who share them to stress certain elements of doctrine and attend to one set of ethical injunctions over another, and styles of organization and ritual often have obvious class connections. So sects and denominations tend to acquire a class identity and within large organizations such as the Catholic Church particular congregations will be seen as 'too posh for the likes of us' and 'rather common'. But the caste impact on Hinduism is more direct, in that many castes have their own deities and rituals. However, the smallness of many Hindu communities in Britain and their limited financial resources mean that British temples are much more likely to be multi-sect, multi-caste, and multi-ethnic than their Gujarati counterparts.

WHAT SIKHS BELIEVE

- A Sikh is someone who believes in *Akal Purakh* (the one immortal God), the ten gurus, the Sikh Scriptures, and the *Gurbani* (the teachings of the ten gurus taken together).

- Sikhism was founded by Guru Nanak Dev, who was born in the Punjab in 1469, and to whom God revealed a religion of peace, love, and brotherhood. Nanak Dev was followed by nine other Gurus. The last Guru vested spiritual authority in the Sikh scriptures and the Sikh community (the *Panth*).

- Sikhs share most of the precepts of Hinduism: though monotheistic, they believe that the one God can be called by many names (including Allah); they believe in reincarnation according to the principle of *karma*; and they view the final goal of man as release from the cycle of rebirth and reabsorption into God.

- In theory Sikhs reject the Hindu divisions of castes. According to tradition, the first five people to be initiated by the tenth guru were all given the name *Singh* (which means Lion) in place of their caste names to signify that break. In practice British Sikhs are organized in caste associations, aim to marry only within their caste, and will even share rituals with Hindus of the same caste.

- Orthodox Sikhs signify their religion by wearing the five 'Ks'—so-called because the Punjabi word for each begins with a K. They wear their hair uncut (often in a turban), a small comb in the hair (to symbolize orderly spirituality), a steel bracelet (to symbolize spiritual allegiance and brotherhood and to remind the wearer to do good), a knee-length undergarment (to symbolize modesty), and a dagger (to symbolize readiness to fight either in self-defence or to protect the weak).

Sikhs

Most British Sikhs came from the Punjab, a region of India which, until the British Raj, was a sovereign Sikh nation and, on British departure, was divided between India and Pakistan. A sizeable minority came via East Africa and other British colonies. There are some 400,000 Sikhs in Britain, which is the largest body outside the Punjab, concentrated in Birmingham, Bradford, Cardiff, Coventry, Glasgow, Leeds, Leicester, and Wolverhampton. There is a large community in Southall in London.

The first *Gurdwara* or place of Sikh worship was opened in Putney in 1911. There are now some 180 *Gurdwaras* in Britain. Like the Muslim mosque and the Hindu temple, the *Gurdwara* is more than a church; it is also a community centre which offers such vital resources as instruction in Punjabi, day centres for the elderly, halls for youth groups, and the like. Although Sikhs pray at home and some may have a room set aside for a copy of the scriptures, congregational worship is regarded as an important part of Sikh life. Although no particular day is holy to the Sikhs, for convenience they follow the Christian habit of holding their main service on a Sunday.

Community Development and Religious Observance

The Muslim, Hindu, and Sikh communities described here all have one thing in common: they are markedly more religious than the host society. After all, they have been recently created by people from countries where religion remains a central part of the culture. Furthermore, the close kinship ties that bind immigrant families to each other and to families in the mother country create considerable social pressure to conform.

Various elements of a third reason for high rates of observance have already been mentioned: religion is socially functional. Ethnic-minority religious centres perform important social roles in addition to their primary religious purpose: a first point of contact for the new immigrant, continuity with the old world, a wealth of friends and potential spouses, an educational centre, and a source of social-welfare provision. They also have a less practical but no less important role in compensating for the socio-psychological strains of being part of a deviant and devalued minority.

As a very rough rule of thumb we can suppose that the religious life of recent migrant communities has gone through two phases and is now entering a third. However devout they may have been personally, the first migrant workers would have been relatively lax because the facilities for leading a religiously orthodox life were not in place and the lack of family meant the absence of one good reason for being observant. Acquiring wives and children led to increased orthodoxy, as relations with them and their relations with others posed the choice of either maintaining traditional gender roles (and the religion that legitimated them) or going 'Western', and most chose the former. The growth of the communities allowed the religious and cultural institutions to be created.

However, a number of circumstances are forcing Hindus, Muslims, and Sikhs, like the Jews before them, to revalue their religious commitments. Because they are pantheistic, Hindus are accustomed to pluralism in belief and ritual, but settlement in Britain has made Muslims and Sikhs aware of the considerable differences within their religions which were less apparent to them in their home setting. Although castes, sects, and traditions attempt, when they are large enough, to create their own institutions, they cannot avoid being confronted with the realization that rituals and beliefs which they take to be normative are not shared by people who claim to follow the same religion. As I suggested in discussing the impact of cultural pluralism on conservative Protestant sects, such awareness of internal diversity is a far greater challenge to the 'taken-for-granted' certainty which makes religion plausible than is the knowledge that there are 'heathens' out there, people quite beyond the pale who share none of your beliefs. The power of inertia is such that old people will continue as they always did, but young Muslims, being faced with alternative expressions of Islam, are forced to question which of those alternatives is right.

Ethnic minorities are also challenged by changes in their religion in other countries. Political conflicts in India and Pakistan, where militant Sikhs have recently and dramatically been pursuing their desire for an independent Sikh homeland, where Hindu nationalists have been attacking Indian Muslims, and where Muslims have been pressing for a more aggressive imposition of Islamic law, have all reverberated around British communities. The political successes of militant Islam in the Middle East as well as South-East Asia offer a mixed message to British Muslims. They can take some pleasure in the advance of their faith but they are also mindful that many Islamic revival movements are highly critical of what they see as later corruptions of the true faith and wish to shed many beliefs and practices that are commonplace among the older generations of Muslims.

Although many New Commonwealth immigrants send their children to their mother country for a period to ensure that the sense of belonging elsewhere is passed on to the next generation, their children are growing up to be British. Even if the mother tongue is enthusiastically embraced, it remains an optional extra which suffers in comparison with English because it is not used when the children go out of the home and the neighbourhood to school or college or work. That Muslims of every ethnic group have always had the rudiments of Arabic as the language in which their religion is conducted to a degree preserves the religious core, but even for Muslims the gradual decline of the mother tongue undermines the wider culture which surrounds and protects that religious core. To a lesser extent the role of Sanskrit provides similar ritual continuity for Hindus, but Sikhs have a greater problem because the mother tongue is also the language of religion. To put it bluntly, many young Sikhs now have trouble understanding the religious rituals they attend because they are conducted in what is at best a second language.

However much traditional patterns of behaviour are stressed at home, they are not reinforced by the surrounding culture. However keen parents are to instruct their children in their religion, it promotes a world-view which gains no implicit support from the wider society. The video is a godsend to all cultural minorities because it allows some doses of the imported culture to be inserted into children's television viewing diet, but modern secular cosmopolitan and permissive culture is pervasive and it is powerful.

Members of ethnic-minority religions need to revalue and redefine their faith in novel and difficult circumstances. We might expect that, as they become better integrated with the Britain that envelops them, their religious commitment will gradually decline, and there are signs of that, but simple assimilation is not inevitable and it is not the most likely outcome. We must remember that integration may not be welcome to the host society. External hostility creates pressure to maintain identity and allegiance, but, because the surrounding society is blind to internal differences, what future generations retain may be very different from the past and present. 'The next generation, the third generation which is now coming up are calling themselves Muslims not Pakistanis or Asians. They are speaking English, their culture is British and they are Muslims. What it means, of course, is that we have decided to stay here in Britain.'[6] There may be a little wishful thinking in this view from an Imam, but it captures the important truth that identity emerges from the *interaction* of the presently distinctive subcultures and the wider society: 'with young Sikhs the situation is somewhat paradoxical; their knowledge of Punjabi and the Sikh religion may be very restricted, but to an increasing extent they are adopting the turban and uncut hair, if not [the rest of] the five K's.'[7] The new identity is likely to be more British and, because the traditional religions stress orthopraxy rather than orthodoxy, more secular. Because the new world is thoroughly individualistic, any assimilation will weaken the social cohesion of the minority communities, but some of that tendency may well be offset by the consequences of hostile racist elements treating members of ethnic minorities as members of a group.

The Culture Clash

Many requirements of the religions discussed here do not create any particular problem because the injunctions affect the lives of individuals in particulars which we regard as a matter of personal preference and which, anyway, are not unique to these religions. Almost all Sikhs and Hindus and all Buddhists are vegetarians, but then so are many Christians. Injunctions against the use of such intoxicants as alcohol and tobacco are common not only among evangelical Protestants and conservative Catholics but among people who have entirely secular reasons for staying off the booze and fags.

However, there remains points of possible conflict, many of them accidental in the sense that laws drafted with no thought for religious sensibilities turn out to conflict with some minority-religion requirement. The 1972 Road Traffic Act required all motorcyclists to wear crash helmets and it took four years of hard campaigning to have turban-wearing Sikhs exempted from its provisions. In 1993 the Strathclyde Police and Regional Council responded to the increasing number of stabbings in the greater Glasgow area by banning knives from schools. A Sikh boy was kept off school for six months until a compromise was worked out that allowed him to wear his *kirpan* sealed in a metal box under his clothes.

The problems that arise from specific religious requirements can often be handled as matters of individual choice. Greater difficulty is caused by general cultural preferences that are at odds with the assumptions of the wider society. A major source of friction between, on the one hand, Muslims, Sikhs, and Hindus, and, on the other,

British culture is the whole issue of gender relations. Like Victorian Christianity, these religions insist that they accord equal respect to men and women but also insist on the segregation of the sexes in many settings and maintain a traditional division of gender roles. Contact between men and women who are not family members is restricted in many ways that to modern Western eyes look like unfair constraints on women. Strict Muslims want women to remain within the home as much as possible and to keep not only their bodies but also their faces covered when in male company. We are then faced with a choice between competing rhetorics of rights. As citizens of a liberal democracy we wish to respect the rights of religious minorities but we also wish to respect the rights of women, which, unlike Muslims and Hindus, we define in universal rather than gender-specific terms.

One sphere in which this tension is particularly acute is education. Sensibly any group with a distinctive culture will be concerned about what is taught to its children, the next generation which must learn and endorse the culture if it is to survive. Minorities can organize their own evening and weekend classes to add their specific elements to the education provided by the public schools, and this is one of the main social functions of mosques, temples, and *gurdwaras*. Where a school is sympathetic, some of what minorities want can be readily incorporated. For example, the Muslim requirement for modesty in women can be met within the conventions of school uniforms by allowing girls to wear thick tights or leggings under school skirts. When Conservative party politicians started talking about the need for greater stress on Christian teachings, religious education looked as though it might become a bone of contention, but the 1994 guidelines seem to be sufficiently generous to accommodate minority interests. However, what cannot so easily be accepted is the general principle of sex segregation.

But, however large that issue looms, it is, I would suggest, merely an instance of a bigger problem that is not obviously amenable to negotiated settlement. Behind the specific points of conflict between ethnic minority religion and the culture of the modern secular society, there is a very general tension, and exploring it will allow us to see clearly a central characteristic of religion in modern societies. It is a simplification, of course, but we can usefully describe modern societies as being marked by a fairly abrupt division between the public and the private. Each sphere has its own values and norms. The public sphere is supposed to be rational and universalistic. What I mean can be easily illustrated with the example of a social benefit such as 'income support'. In pre-modern societies, it was quite acceptable (indeed expected) that those who controlled a scare resource would use it to further their own interests and those of their family, close connections, and at its widest 'their people'. In the eighteenth and nineteenth centuries, it was normal to give charity only to those who met a variety of requirements unrelated to their needs: professing to be of good Christian character, for example. Nowadays we would regard giving income support only to co-religionists as discrimination. We expect the clerks who control access to such benefits to follow a set of universal rules, designed only for the matter in hand, in deciding entitlement, irrespective of how they feel about this or that claimant. Everyone has the vote. Employers are supposed to consider only suitability for the job in deciding who to hire. Housing authorities charge rents according to the nature of the property, not the occupant. Supermarkets do not vary prices according to the religion, gender, or age of the customer.

In the public sphere we are supposed to be task-oriented and instrumental and we have developed a body of law which aims to constrain our ability to be otherwise. This increasing constraint has been accompanied by increased permissiveness in the private sphere. What we do at home, at leisure, is our business. Indeed we are encouraged to see the home as a place for expressive spontaneous activity and it is here that we 'do' religion.

Except for a very small number of radical sects, most Christians have happily colluded in this division of the modern world into the rational and instrumental public sphere and the expressive and affective private sphere. Requirements that operated at the community or social level have been conveniently dropped or their religious basis has been replaced by an argument for general social benefit. Thus the rapidly diminishing band of opponents of drinking and gambling now offers secular arguments against those evils, and the Lord's Day Observance Society fights its losing battle against Sunday shopping on grounds of social welfare, not divine ordinance. By happy coincidence, what is required of someone living the Christian life has been reworked so as to confine it to the private sphere.

But, to return to a theme of the first chapter, the British road to the secularization of public life has been very different from the US model. The US constitution explicitly creates a secular state in that it prevents the state endorsing any religion or prohibiting an individual's right to the free exercise of religious preferences. In the evolution of church–state relations in Britain, the state churches lost the guts of their privileged position but retained some of the outward appearance. By the start of this century the Nonconformist denominations were reluctant to press for the final extermination of the hated religious establishment because by then secular forces were so strong that further attacks on the privileges of the state churches would be seen as attacks on religion *per se*. We thus ended up with a fudged accommodation. The Catholic Church and the Church of England retain schools which they manage but which the state funds. Some bishops have seats in the House of Lords. The monarch remains head of the Church of England and of the Church of Scotland. Blasphemy remains a criminal offence. Religious broadcasting is given television and radio air time well out of proportion with the size of the church-going population. However, the key characteristic of the British church–state accommodation, which all the players know but never explicitly state, is that it only works because nobody takes religion too seriously! A rabbi and a bishop can alternate on Radio 4's *Thought for the Day* because both confine themselves to a vague middle way of consensus moral values and toleration.

And into this fudge walk a number of religious minorities which take the specific claims and requirements of their religion very seriously. That in itself is a problem for a secular society, but it is exacerbated by the encouragement to religious particularism that the fudge gives. As we saw in the reactions to the Ayatollah Khomeini's death sentence on the novelist Salman Rushdie in 1989, Muslims can ask why we have blasphemy laws if we are not prepared to use them to prevent insults to Muhammad. They can also ask why, if the state funds Catholic and Anglican church schools, it will not fund Muslim schools. The correct answer is that we allow access to devices for promoting religious beliefs and values only to those groups which have accepted that religion should be confined to the private sphere.

The difficulty that ethnic minority religions have to face is that, whereas the various strands within Christianity have changed slowly over centuries as the modern secular society has emerged—a secular society whose accommodations with religion have been shaped by those strands—most ethnic minorities have moved abruptly from a society in which their religion was dominant and all-pervasive to an environment in which they form a small deviant minority, radically at odds with the world around them. It may be acceptable to threaten blaspheming authors with death in Bangladesh or Iran, where there is considerable agreement both on what counts as blasphemy and on the seriousness of the offence. In a culturally diverse secular society, it is not possible or acceptable.

Although, as already noted, adherents of ethnic-minority religions have the added characteristic that they may suffer the additional disadvantage of racial discrimination, the choice that faces them in thinking about the nature of their religion is much the same as that faced by the various strands of the Christian tradition. To put it in the terms used in Chapter One, where cultural diversity prevents a religion existing in the 'church' form, it can, if the social circumstances permit, retreat into the shell of the 'sect', or it can become more tolerant and inclusive and more like a 'denomination'.

Further Reading

Useful introductions to ethnic-minority religions in Britain can be found in the various contributions to Paul Badham (ed.), *Religion, State and Society in Modern Britain* (Lampeter: Edwin Mellen, 1989), and in Paul Weller (ed.), *Religions in the UK: A Multi-Faith Directory* (Derby: University of Derby and the Inter-Faith Network for the United Kingdom, 1994). For detailed studies of particular communities, see Ken Pryce, *Endless Pressure: A Study of West Indian Life-Styles in Bristol* (Harmondsworth, Middx.: Penguin, 1979); Rohit Barot (ed.), *Religion and Ethnicity: Minorities and Social Change in the Metropolis* (Kampen, The Netherlands: Pharos, 1993); Sewa Singh Kalsi, *The Evolution of a Sikh Community in Britain* (Leeds: Department of Theology and Religious Studies, University of Leeds, 1992); and Jorgen Nielsen, *Muslims in Western Europe* (Edinburgh: Edinburgh University Press, 1992).

Chapter Four

New Religions and the New Age

There are three roads to cultural diversity. The first chapter described the fragmentation of Britain's dominant Christian culture into competing variations on the common themes. Radically different beliefs and practices may be brought by migrants from lands where what appear to us as deviant innovations are orthodox; that is the case with the minority religions described in the previous chapter. But innovation may also arise from within a stable population when the once-dominant culture has become so weakened that people feel free to search the global supermarket of cultures for new ideas and new perspectives. This chapter is concerned first with the 'new religious movements' that attracted so much attention in the 1970s and then with the New Age spirituality of the 1980s and 1990s. For the sake of simplicity, the two are treated sequentially, although, as will become clear, there is no abrupt or radical division between the religious innovations of the two periods.

New Religions

The late 1960s and early 1970s saw a flowering of new cults and sects. Some were Hindu and Buddhist imports from the Orient: Rajneeshism, Transcendental Meditation (TM), the Meher Baba Movement, the Divine Light Mission, Krishna Consciousness, and the Healthy-Happy-Holy movement of Yogi Bhajan (a variant of Sikhism) were the best known. Others were psychotherapies that bordered on the religious or which became progressively more spiritual over the decade: Werner Erhard's Erhard Seminar Training ('est') and its spin-offs Psycho-synthesis and Insight, Arica, Bioenergetics, Silva Mind Control, Scientology, Kerista, Primal Therapy, Co-Counselling, and Rebirthing are examples. All offered techniques for improving the 'self', but they differed from conventional psychotherapy in asserting its perfectibility.

We could sort these groups by the religious tradition of their roots but their most interesting features cut across those lines. Patterns of recruitment, appeal, and evolution are better explained by their general orientation to the world than by the specific religious culture from which they come. At its simplest, some of the new religions *rejected* the world while some positively *affirmed* it.

World-Rejecting Movements

One of the best known (or most notorious) of the new religions is the Unification Church (UC), founded in Korea in 1954 by Sun Myung Moon, the son of a Korean convert to evangelical Presbyterianism. The movement appeared in California in the early 1960s but did not really grow until the early 1970s, when Moon himself moved to the United States. Moon believed that Christianity needed to be superseded because its disunity had undermined morality and the churches themselves. He saw his role as completing Christ's unfinished work by establishing the Kingdom of Heaven on earth.

The Moonies view the mundane secular world as an evil place ruined by the pursuit of material gain, to be avoided as much as possible until one leaves it for good, and, as part of that avoidance, they are thoroughly ascetic or self-denying. Unlike the members of the Hare Krishna movement (or ISKCON), whose members shared an *ashram*, the Moonies did not live communally, but unmarried adherents were expected to devote their energies to promoting the movement and that usually meant working full time for it for very small rewards. They did not smoke, drink, or take drugs. Although they developed the unusual practice of having mass weddings of members presided over by Revd and Mrs Moon (who often selected the partners), the Moonies had old-fashioned views of the purpose of sex and an exalted view of the nuclear family, where relationships were meant to mirror those between the Heavenly Father and his earthly children. Moonies took vows of premarital celibacy and believed that sexual intercourse should be permitted only within monogamous heterosexual marriage.

The world-rejecting movements were demanding. Self-denial is a high price to pay and followers were expected to pay it, with a change in their lives drastic enough to be described as 'conversion'. There was also a literal high price. Many recruits signalled the break with their old identities by giving all their capital to the movement. Strange beliefs might be tolerated, but such un-American activity seriously offended middle America. The world-rejecting movement typically accorded a very low value to the human self. As in traditional Christianity, the self is essentially sinful and is improved only by being subordinated to some higher authority.

One very common response to the world-rejecting new religious movements was to suppose their leaders possessed mysterious powers of 'mind control' and 'brainwashing'. With hindsight it is clear that such stories owed much to ex-members having to explain to themselves and to others how they could, for a short time, have believed things that they later found very strange. The idea that they had been manipulated was attractive because it freed them from responsibility for their now inexplicable actions. What thoroughly undermines the notion of mind control is the evidence of just how unsuccessful new religious movements were in controlling minds and in recruiting. Eileen Barker followed a large number of young people from their first contact with the Moonies through to either departure or full membership. Table 4.1 shows the percentages who progressed through various degrees of contact. Very very few of those who were keen enough to attend a two-day workshop (and that was a very small fraction of those whom the Moonies contacted) actually pursued their interest. At most, only 3.5 per cent were still members four years later.

Table 4.1 Unification Careers, London, 1979 (%)

2-day workshop: start	100
2-day workshop: finish	85
7-day workshop: start	30
7-day workshop: finish	25
21-day workshop: start	18
21-day workshop: finish	15
Agree to affiliate to UC (inc. 'home church' members and full-time students)	13
Actually join for more than 1 week	10
Still affiliated after 1 year	7
Still affiliated after 2 years	5
Max. percentage still full-time UC on 1 January 1983	3.5

Note: N = 1,017.

Source: Eileen Barker, The Making of a Moonie: Brainwashing or Choice? (Oxford: Basil Blackwell, 1984), 146.

World-Affirming Movements

Although media attention focused on the more sectarian world-rejecting movements, the most popular new religions were very different in character. The world-affirming movements generally lacked most of the features associated with 'religion': they had no church, no collective ritual of worship, no fully developed theology, and no ethical system (in the sense of general principles which tell us what to want and how to behave). They were happy with much of the secular world and had a generally positive attitude to humankind and to the 'self'. In an extension of that American strain of 'can-do' optimism that produced Norman Vincent Peale's *Power of Positive Thinking*, the world-affirming movements argued that people are not so much evil as *restricted*. We are all extremely powerful but we need to learn to exploit our potential. Particularly we need to be taught to free ourselves from the internal constraints that are the legacy of the way our parents raised us.

There are two very different sorts of world-affirming movements: those which add a spiritual dimension to what had been a Western secular psychotherapy and those which tailor an initially oriental product for Western sensibilities. An example of the former is Insight. Insight trainers believe that inside all of us is a 'centre' which already knows everything we want to know. We can be liberated from fear, guilt, and anxiety, from self-limiting images that make us feel unworthy, and from the sense of ourselves as victims. The aim of the training is to get people to accept total responsibility for their lives, and central to that is learning to complement reasoning with feeling, the mind with the heart.

The techniques for unlocking human potential and liberating the self vary from movement to movement but many involve role-playing designed to force people to confront their inhibitions, discuss their problems openly, and mix freely with others. That is, they are modelled on the now quite common form of the encounter group.

The best-known and most popular example of an eastern religious innovation which was successfully modified for Western sensibilities is Transcendental Meditation (or TM). TM was brought to the West by the Hindu Mahareshi Mahesh Yogi in the early 1950s, but the West only noticed in 1968, when, prompted by George Harrison (whose involvement with Indian religion lasted more than a weekend), the Beatles and some of the Rolling Stones travelled to India to visit the Mahareshi.

TM is a meditational technique taught to those who are initiated in a brief ceremony in which the initiator conveys to the new mediator a personal mantra. The person then meditates on that mantra for twenty minutes morning and evening every day. Although meditation in its original Hindu context is usually associated with a rigorous programme of discipleship and world-renunciation, TM is now promoted as a technique for becoming more efficient and effective in the here and now. As we can see from an advertisement which appeared in the *Independent*, the primary appeal is to instrumentalism and the ease of acquiring the technique is stressed. Claims to supernatural powers have not been entirely dropped, but they have been shifted to the background. Meditators can, if they wish, 'upgrade' by enrolling in the Siddhis programme, which teaches such special skills as the ability to levitate.

TRANSCENDENTAL MEDITATION

Transcendental Meditation is a natural and effective technique which relaxes, revitalises and recharges your energy to get more out of life. It leaves you feeling positive, alert and clear with the calmness and inner contentment to tackle life with enthusiasm. It protects you from stress and future ill-health.

TM has been verified by independent scientific research and is recommended by hundreds of doctors in Britain.

A simple technique to develop your true potential, it requires no belief or change in lifestyle. It takes just a few minutes every day but will work for you for a lifetime.

Source: Independent, 21 July 1992.

Although it is thoroughly individualistic, TM believes that the supernatural powers it channels have beneficial social consequences. There is the cumulative effect—if enough individuals get saved, then the world will change—but TM also holds that, if a critical mass of people meditate regularly, the level of cosmic consciousness will rise sufficiently to have benefits far beyond what can be created by the sum of the individuals. Such claims were elaborated and widely advertised in 1992, when the Natural Law Party fielded some 300 candidates in a general election. The Party's manifesto promised that raised cosmic consciousness would solve unemployment, crime, and all the other ills for which the conventional parties were suggesting more mundane solutions.

We can characterize the typical world-affirming new religion as follows. It does not renounce the world; in principle the world is good. What is not good is that more people cannot enjoy the good life because their personality (rather than social circumstances) stops them fulfilling their potential. The movement offers techniques which free the inner self and empower the individual. Not much is required by way of commitment. The movement may be given some continuity and stability by a higher level of knowledge which is revealed only to a select group of extra-committed devotees. Thus TM, the Church of Scientology (which was founded by L. Ron Hubbard on his theory of Dianetics), and the movement of guru Shree Bhagwan Rajneesh had a strong inner circle of practitioners who worked for the movement and who might sensibly be described as followers, but most people participated as consumers. They learnt the basic meditation techniques, they spent a couple of weekends at a conference centre, they took some evening classes, and they continued with their conventional lives. And, as we saw in the TM advertisement, not much is required by way of change of belief. Although the inner core of adepts will be well versed in the justifications for the therapies and empowering techniques, it is not necessary for ordinary clients or consumers to understand or be committed to these.

World-affirming movements differ in the extent to which there is some power other than the self, something which, if it is not sufficiently personal to be worshipped, one can at least merge with in an ecstatic experience. Whether or not Rajneeshism and TM are 'theistic' is rather a matter of which layer of the onion one happens to be peeling off at the time. In the Hinduism from which they grew, the supernatural power can present itself or be seen as a God or Gods (Vishnu or Shiva, for example), but even these entities are 'really' only the embodiment of a force which, while it has moral purpose, is none the less impersonal. Such a force is clearly a long way from the personal God of Christianity or Islam, but it still has enough of a presence to give Rajneeshism and TM a more spiritual feel than such explicitly self-oriented movements as est and Exegesis. In those, the experience of God that is offered is of the God within. This difference reflects their origins: the former an industrialized version of eastern mysticism; the latter a mysticized version of industrial therapy. They meet in drawing on some notion of a cosmic consciousness to explain how the individual self may have powers and potentials beyond its obvious material constraints, but it is the self, the I, the me, which is the main focus of attention.

We might imagine that world-affirming new religious movements would have a major problem with their claims to empower people: the real world would refute them at every turn. Much of what happens to us is outside our control. Our ability to alter the circumstances in which we work and live is slight. Personal qualities may raise or lower our chances of getting a job, for example, but they do so only within the constraints of the labour-market. We might suppose then that those who turn to world-affirming movements to make themselves more effective and powerful would quickly become disillusioned, but the movements that have endured have managed to resolve the problem by encouraging an interesting flexibility in what counts as success. Soka Gakkai Buddhists believe that chanting produces that which one asks for in chanting. Much of what is desired is sufficiently a matter of mind ('being more content with the world') that to believe it will work is itself almost a guarantee of success, but people also chant for very specific goals. However, when they fail to attain those, they can readily interpret the result as even better than the ones they originally sought. The marriage does not work out, but in retrospect separation is seen as an opportunity to come to terms with oneself.

To put it rather harshly, movements which promise empowerment often actually deliver acceptance of the status quo. As Werner Erhard put it in an est seminar: 'Life is always perfect just the way it is. When you realise that, then no matter how strongly it may appear to be otherwise, you know that whatever is happening right now will turn out to be all right. Knowing this you are in a position to begin mastering life.'[1] Or is that passively accepting life?

The Significance of New Religious Movements

How important were the new religious movements as cultural innovations? Though exotic and always good for a tabloid horror story, the world-rejecting ones were numerically insignificant. Because some organizations keep no records, some keep their records secret, and others have unhelpful ways of calculating 'members', it is hard to be precise, but the grounds for supposing numerical insignificance can be readily illustrated. In 1989 the Unification Church claimed only 350 full-time core members, a further 100 'practising' members, and about 8,000 'associates' (and less than one in ten of these had any continuing contact with the organization). There were about 150 Emissaries of Divine Light, sixty of whom live in their Cotswold community. There were only some 300 full-time devotees of the Hare Krishna movement. Set against the shrinkage of the Christian denominations and sects, such figures are trivial. Brierley's studies suggest that each year between 1975 and 1989 the Christian denominations lost 28,000 adults, mostly through failing to recruit replacements for those who died. Ninety per cent of British adults do not attend church and 80 per cent are not church members.

From a total adult population of 48 million that leaves a market for new religions of 38 million people. Even if the best guesses of new-movement involvement grossly under-represent it, it is obvious that only a minute proportion of those who are free to do so have taken the opportunity to explore radically different forms of spirituality.

The world-affirming movements, because they spread thinner, spread further. TM estimates that some 6,000 people attend a four-day course each year and some 2,500 take the more advanced 'TM-Siddhis' programme. The Church of Scientology claims that some 100,000 people have taken its courses since the 1950s, but only a minute fraction of these continue with the sort of commitment we think of as conventional church membership. About 4,000 people have been initiated into Nichiren Shoshu Buddhism. Because such movements by and large either reconcile adherents to their place in the world or help them to perform better in their present roles, their impact is limited to the personalities of the small number of people involved. This should not be dismissed; many people are happier and more content because of their involvement with Soka Gakkai or TM or Insight, but equally we should appreciate the highly privatized nature of the consequences of such involvement. The old religious movements changed their worlds; the world-affirming new religious movements slightly altered the psyches of their small numbers of consumers.

But the new religious movements might still be significant for our thinking about the demand for religion. They are often cited as evidence that religious seeking remains widespread and hence that modernity does not undermine the possibility of faith in the supernatural. Again the numbers are relevant and what they show is a number of spiritual seekers that, when set against the continuing slow growth of such nineteenth-century movements as the Jehovah's Witnesses or the Mormons, is small and, when set against the general decline in the Christian churches, is trivial. And again the difference in popularity of world-rejecting and world-affirming movements is important. Had it been the former type—the Moonies, the Divine Light Mission, or ISKCON—that had been more popular, this would have been good evidence to take seriously the idea that, because human needs are constant and only supernatural religion can satisfy them, the collapse of one religious tradition should be followed by the rise of the compensating alternative. Unfortunately, it was those movements which were least traditionally religious, most individualistic, and most directed to helping consumers either succeed in the material world or become reconciled to their present circumstances which proved the most popular and most enduring.

The New Age

'New Age' is a term used loosely to describe a very wide range of beliefs and practices which became popular in the 1980s. Many have their roots in the esoteric culture of the late nineteenth century, while others are extensions of the world-affirming new religions and human-potential movements discussed above. Some of the new religions of the 1970s—primarily those of the world-affirming type—were at the cultic end of the continuum, but the most prominent were sects. In the New Age, the balance is reversed; most of the movements are cults and even to call them movements is to imply a degree of cohesion and structure which they do not possess. The most common ways in which activity in this milieu is organized is through the 'client cult' and the 'audience cult'.

The client cult is structured around the individual relationship between a consumer and a purveyor. Typical are the alternative thera-pists who advertise their services in an appropriate magazine or the bulletin board of a health-food shop and provide individual consulta-tions for a fee. Audience cults are generally structured around the mass distribution of the word, spoken and printed. The circulatory system of the New Age body is made up of books, magazines, audio cassettes, and public lectures. If there is personal contact, it is usually in the form of a lecture-and-workshop circuit. Promoters of particular revelations or techniques advertise their meetings, present their insights and thera-pies, and move on. Such touring 'stars' complement the routine and regular meetings organized by such bodies as the Society for Psychical Research ('Clairvoyance—How Far can we See?', and 'Alien Contact, the Inner Dimension of the UFO Mystery') and the London Earth Mysteries Circle ('Reclaiming our Heritage', 'Earth Mysteries and Magnetism', and 'UFOs and Psychic Phenomena').

The amorphous nature of the New Age makes the notion of member-ship redundant. We have to ask to what extent are people influenced by the New Age rather than how many New Agers there are. There have been a few attempts to use surveys to do this, but these suffer from all the obvious problems of unambiguously identifying and measuring signs of New Age belief and behaviour. A 1992 survey (see Table 4.2) asked almost 2,000 teenagers (divided into a school group and a church group) 'Have you ever been involved in any of the following?' and listed eight occult practices. The findings were reported as a matter of urgent concern, but one has to wonder what the respondents thought was

Table 4.2 Teenagers Involved in Occult Practices, England, 1992 (%)

'Have you ever been involved in any of the following?'	School	Church
Ouija	26	8
Astrology	18	10
Tarot	13	6
Hypnosis	5	3
Crystals	3	2
Reflexology	3	2
Channelling	3	1
I Ching	2	1

Source: Peter Brierley, *Reaching and Keeping Teenagers* (London: Christian Research Association, 1993), 80.

meant by 'involved'. It is also worth noting that those elements of occultism which had been most sampled—if indeed that is what the question tested—were those that date from the Victorians' interest in the occult and are well established as part of our cultural wallpaper. The New Age novelties—channelling and the use of crystals—are almost unknown.

However, there are less ambiguous markers of new activity in the New Age milieu. The annual London Mind, Body, and Spirit convention began in 1977 as a one-day event with only a small number of exhibitors. In the late 1980s it was extended to five days. In 1993 over a hundred individuals and organizations presented their products or ideas from stalls in the main hall, and there was sufficient interest in the lectures and workshops for the convention to run over ten days.

The New Age's reliance on the printed word gives us a surer way of illustrating the popularity of New Age ideas. It is obvious to any browser in British bookshops that far more space is now devoted to what is usually called 'Mind, Body, and Spirit' than to Christianity. Waterstone's shop in Aberdeen has some 70 metres of shelves of New Age books, but fits its more traditional Christian titles into 5 metres. In the twenty years between 1970 and 1990 the total number of new titles published in the United Kingdom just about doubled. The number of published books that were 'religious' (including the occult) increased by close to that proportion, but the occult section grew by 150 per cent. Table 4.3 shows the relative proportions. As good a sign as any that the market is large is the entry into it in the late 1980s of all the major publishing houses, with specialist labels for their New Age offerings. Thus Penguin has its

Table 4.3 Books Published, United Kingdom, 1928–1990

Year	Religious titles (inc. occult) as % of all titles	Occult titles as % of all titles	Occult titles as % of religious titles
1928	6.8	0.22	3.3
1940	4.7	0.36	7.7
1950	5.7	0.31	5.6
1960	5.2	0.29	5.6
1970	3.7	0.49	13.4
1980	3.6	0.54	15.0
1990	3.7	0.64	17.3

Source: Peter Brierley, *A Century of British Christianity: Historical Statistics 1900–1985 with Projections to 2000* (Research Monograph 14; London: MARC Europe, 1985).

Arkana imprint. HarperCollins has Aquarius, Mandala, and Thorsons imprints, and Random Century has Rider and Shambala.

One of the dominant characteristics of New Age thought is its eclecticism. One of Element's most successful publishing lines is a series of titles called 'Elements of . . .'. The nouns that follow demonstrate both the diversity of the New Age and the lack of any attempt to define a canon of acceptable revelations. Current topics in the series include: Alchemy, Astrology, Buddhism, Christian Symbolism, Creation Myth, Dreamwork, Earth Mysteries, Feng Sui, Herbalism, Human Potential, Meditation, Mysticism, Natural Magic, Pendulum Dowsing, Prophecy, Psychosynthesis, Shamanism, Sufism, Taoism, Aborigine Tradition, Chakras, The Goddess, The Grail Tradition, Greek Tradition, Qabalah, Visualization, Zen.

With eclecticism comes a diffuseness that means that there are few clear divisions and boundaries, few organizations, but rather a milieu in which people acquire and absorb a variety of beliefs and practices that they combine into their own pockets of culture and attend to with differing degrees of seriousness. For some, it is no more than reading a book and entertaining an idea; for others it is a change of world-view and direction comparable to conversion in more traditional religions. Consider astrology. A very small number of people make their livings as professional astrologers. Around them is a layer of people who strongly believe that the solar system is the symbol of a living energy pattern and that its arrangement tells us something useful about human personality and the course of events. They will use 'birth maps' and birth signs as a guide to interpreting the behaviour of themselves and others, and will consider the lie of the planets before making major decisions. There are also those who read horoscopes with no conviction that they are useful but with the general supposition that it does no harm. In this circle there are a very large number of people. The fourth best-selling book of 1993, behind three novels, was *1994 Horoscopes*, which sold 480,000 copies in the United Kingdom, which is about one for every 100 adults.

Beyond that circle we have those who glance at horoscopes in popular magazines and newspapers and who have acquired enough information to be able to describe people in terms of the characteristics imputed to their birth sign: 'She's a typical Arian!' A 1982 survey in Leeds showed 75 per cent of people saying they looked at their horoscopes but only 19 per cent saying they 'believed in it'.[2]

The Themes of the New Age

In the introduction to a beginner's New Age reader William Bloom summarizes New Age thought under four main headings. *New Science/New Paradigm* includes 'all the new theories which are reworking our intellectual understanding of the structures of life'. Such theories have in common the belief that the basis for conventional science is wrong. The world is not made up of 'tangible bits and pieces following certain reliable laws of interaction' but is instead composed of matter and energy 'connected and formed in invisible ways that we are only just beginning to understand'.[3] The interconnectedness of everything informs New Age attitudes to health and healing. In place of the medical-science treatment of symptoms and organs, there is attention to the 'whole person'. Then there is *New Ecology*, which is concerned with our responsibilities to the earth. Third, and this is where we come back to the human-potential movement, there is the *New Psychology*, which, like Scientology, claims to be able to liberate our real and vast potential so that we become 'integrated, fulfilled and completely loving human beings'.[4]

Underlying these three themes is the *New Spirituality*. Bloom, himself a practising magician, says: 'for me the hallmark of the New Age is the power of *Spiritual Dynamics*.'[5]

New Science

For outsiders, one of the most startling features of the New Age is its apparent deviation from the rational scientific world-view which dominates Western culture. The first clash concerns how we discover knowledge. This summary simplifies, of course, but what allowed conventional science and medicine to break out of such pre-modern dead ends as alchemy, astrology, and the theory of the four humours was their insistence on experimentation, observation, and testing. And the field for observation is restricted to the mundane material world. New Agers tend to have little interest in conventional notions of testing. That one or two people assert that a therapy worked for them is enough to establish its efficacy. New paradigms are not 'discovered' by painstakingly trying to explain observations that do not fit with existing well-established theories, but by revelation and by returning to archaic traditions.

New Agers will happily believe that a book apparently written by Jane Roberts is actually a 'channelled' message from 'Seth', 'an energy personality essence no longer focused in physical reality'.[6] They will happily believe that the ability to channel the thoughts of spirit guides, 'ascended masters', long-dead historical figures, and even animal and vegetable spirits, is now widely distributed. They will believe that in the early 1980s 'Alper' (the founder of the Arizona Metaphysical Society) received three volumes of channelled instruction about the lost ancient civilization of Atlantis. According to Alper's source, the Atlanteans had a crystal technology that allowed them to power their cities and mass-transportation systems from a very large central power crystal. Alper's detailed channellings about the use of crystals for psychic healing and personal growth were extremely influential in promoting the New Age interest in them.

Tradition is also a major legitimator of New Age ideas and therapies. By reasoning backwards from the observation that modern societies have many defects, New Agers conclude that pre-modern cultures must be morally and ethically superior. Tibetans, Eskimos, Native Americans, and Aborigines are then invested not only with superior social mores but also with great insight into the workings of the material world.

There are people in the New Age milieu who are keen to prove their case to sceptical scientists (the proponents of parapsychology, for example), but the dominant attitude is best described as having it both ways. Most often the new idea is supposed to be plausible because it is 'traditional', but one also finds the language of science being invoked wherever possible. Hodgkinson's *Spiritual Healing*, a sweeping review and endorsement of the field, has a chapter called 'The Scientific Rationale'. In so far as the New Age is hostile to any facet of science, it is the supposed close-mindedness and authoritarianism of the professional scientific and medical communities which are criticized.

Especially in promoting their alternative models of the body and the psyche, many New Agers stay fairly close to the modern consensus by confining their interests and their claims to areas which might plausibly be accommodated within conventional theories of causation, even if they are not tested in conventional ways or to the extent which conventional science and medicine would demand. For example, though there is no evidence that the body's healing processes are assisted by magnetism, we have enough experience of radiography and electric-shock therapy at least to imagine magno-therapy being assimilated to conventional models of the body. However, there are strands of the 'New Science'—actually the old occult traditions repackaged—which are so radically at odds with conventional thought that no such accommodation is imaginable. Obvious examples are astrology, witchcraft, and magic. If spells work then science is wrong!

New Ecology

New Agers are Green. The Findhorn community first came to public notice because of the founders' success in vegetable growing, done not with fertilizers but with guidance from Eileen Caddy's inner voice and Dorothy Mclean's conversations with plant spirits. Alongside its human-potential work, environmental concerns remain central to life at Findhorn. As funds have allowed, the old caravans which were the first residences have been replaced by high-insulation buildings made from wood from sustainable forestry projects. Firms developing and marketing insulation and wind generators have been assisted by the Findhorn Foundation. However, New Age Greenery differs from its mundane counterpart in two important respects. First, environmental problems (and their solutions) are closely linked to personal problems:

The root cause is a gross distortion of the human relationship with the earth we live on, caused by the increasing stimulation of material desire. Thus the real solution requires a major personal and collective re-evaluation of the meaning of human life on earth, and of the source of happiness. More sensitive, inwardly directed people make less demands on natural resources and have a much greater appreciation of the wonder of human interaction with the planet.[7]

Secondly, the planet is seen as an organism. We know that elements of our physical environment interact to form something like self-regulating systems: for example, the ozone layer plays an important part in maintaining the temperature of the earth. New Agers have taken the system model one step further to suppose that the earth is really an animate object, a 'super organism' that James Lovelock called Gaia, after the Greek Goddess of Earth. The secular Green protects the environment out of self-interest; the New Age Green does so out of respect for a superior being.

Environmentalism raises an interesting issue of outlook within the New Age. On the one hand, it is critical of aspects of the modern world, especially those such as pollution that can be seen as the side-effects of greed and over-consumption, and in that sense the New Age is 'alternative', but there is little of the blanket condemnation of the present world found in out-and-out world-rejecting new religions. In the astrologer's version, the life span of the world forms a Great Year of twelve months, each composed of 2,160 years and described by the astrological sign that gives us a clue as to the character of that era. Stonehenge was built at the start of the Age of Aries. Christ's birth marks the beginning of the Piscean Age and we stand at the birth of the Age of Aquarius, an unprecedently fruitful time which will be characterized by creativity and spontaneity. Although there are social and economic problems, the human self is perfectible and improving.

New Psychology and New Spirituality

In describing such therapies as that offered by est as self-*religions*, Heelas correctly observed the tendency of once-secular human-potential movements to become increasingly spiritual. One facet of the claim that the self is potentially or actually perfect is its indestructibility. The New Age takes for granted reincarnation, which even in Christian circles is tending to replace the traditional view of a fixed heaven and hell to which individuals go on death. Without wishing to suggest which (if any) of the two visions is correct, I would point out two features of reincarnation which make it more attractive than the Christian conception to modern minds. First, it asserts the central importance of 'me'! The Christian notion of enduring in perfect and eternal peace in the company of God keeps the human soul subordinate to God and that will not do for our assertive individualism. Secondly, it allows notions of justice and consolation to survive the disappearance of God. Even the Christian has trouble understanding how bad things can happen to good people and has to fall back on the unsatisfactory notion of God's inscrutability. The atheist is saddled with the unsatisfying conclusion that there is no justice to life, and no consolation for suffering. By supposing that the soul returns to earth, the believer in reincarnation can hope that a person's desserts in this life are either a fitting reward for past lives or will be made up by a better life next time.

Just as reincarnation allows immortality without a traditional God figure, so New Age spirituality allows for Godless divine revelations. In the 1960s Eileen Caddy received daily 'messages'.

I could sit and meditate for a long time and nothing would come, but as soon as my pen touched the paper it was like switching on an electric current. The words flowed. I was told: 'I work through each of you in different ways. You know when you need guidance from Me, you can receive it instantaneously. Like a flashing of lightning it is there. You can find the answer immediately; therefore you hold great responsibilities in your hands.'[8]

Eileen Caddy initially regarded her revelations as coming from God, rather traditionally conceived. Later she came to see the source as being her higher self: 'There is no separation between ourselves and God, there is only "I am". I am the guidance. It took me many years to realise this.'[9] In the 1970s and 1980s it became more common for channellers to conceptualize their source in highly abstract terms as 'an energy vortex' or some such, but also to give the source a personal name and even imbue it with quasi-personal characteristics. 'Bartholomew', who is channelled by Mary-Margaret Moore, gives advice on such diverse topics as sex, AIDS, group souls, emotional detachment, ego surrender, and prayer. In the *New Age Almanac* entry for Moore, there is an interesting coda which hints at the social composition of her audience: 'Today Moore channels Bartholomew in a variety of locations around the globe that Bartholomew considers to have transformative power. Fans of Bartholomew travel to these points as a group, under the auspices of Inward Bound Tours.'[10]

The Social Origins of Religious Innovation

Who joined the 1970s new religious movements, or, to put it in terms of social structures and cultural changes, what created the conditions for their emergence? The first answers are straightforward. The decline of the mainstream churches and the erosion of the cultural authority of Christianity left a large hole in the market. Secondly, we can note that the vast majority of those who joined the world-rejecting new religions were young people. The increasing prosperity of the economy had lengthened the gap between leaving the family of one's birth and taking on the full adult responsibilities of a family. The Moonies recruited people hanging around bus stations, because their greatest appeal was to young people who were, in the grander sense, 'hanging around', between the roles of child and adult. It was precisely such people who, in the counter-culture of the 1960s and early 1970s, reacted against the dehumanization of the public world. Through political protest, the hippie movement, and the commune movement, young people sought to transform or re-create the world in which they lived. But political protest faced severe repression, and hippie culture and the commune movement largely disintegrated under the impact of drugs and exploitation. Young people committed to a sense that the world could be radically created anew came to see that the transformation they sought could not be achieved solely by human effort. Some had been led towards a more spiritual and mystical view of the world as a result of their drug experiences. By the early 1970s, then, many young people in America and Europe were available for a movement which claimed that some divine agency or power was poised to intervene in the world, that the millennium would be brought about by supernatural means if people would commit themselves zealously to the endeavour. The failure of the counter-culture was thus the principal source of recruits to the world-rejecting new religions.

The world-affirming religions generally recruited an older clientele and their appeal can be understood as a response to the *rationalization* of the modern world. Rationalization is the process whereby life has become organized in terms of instrumental considerations: the concern with technical efficiency, the maximization of calculability and predictability, and the subordination of nature to human purposes. Rationalization carries in its wake what Weber, in quoting Schiller, liked to call 'the disenchantment of the world': a loss of a sense of magic, mystery, prophecy, and the sacred.[11]

Rationalization greatly affects our private as well as our public lives. The family is separated from production; children are separated from adults (in schools and leisure pursuits); where we live is separated from where we work. Modern life is so fragmented that many people find it increasingly difficult to draw on their public roles for a satisfying and fulfilling sense of identity. Many jobs have become routine and mechanized, losing intrinsic interest and satisfaction. Moreover, achievement—what one can do rather than who one is—has become a major preoccupation for people whose image of how they should live, derived from the mass media, leads them to believe that comfort, happiness, and satisfactory relationships are achievable by everyone. Old community structures have broken down, and mobility, social and geographical, makes it increasingly difficult to re-create them in the anonymous world of the city.

Our society creates widespread aspirations for power, status, personal attractiveness, happiness, and the like but distributes these (or the means to gain them) unequally among the population. For those people who find the idea of the supernatural at all plausible but whose interests are focused on the here and now rather than on the next life, the world-affirming new religions offer

a promise to enhance the individual's capacity for rational action by religious means that transcend whatever educational or socialization facilities characterize the wider society, and ... to teach the individual the potency of extra-rational agencies and facilities that will allow him to transcend the merely rational with a superior and arcane wisdom.[12]

The new movements provided the recipe, technique, or knowledge required to reduce the gap between aspiration and actuality. Either, in such movements as TM or Scientology, people would learn to increase their abilities so as to be able to achieve their goals or, in such movements as est or the Neo-Sannyas movement of Bhagwan Shree Rajneesh, people would learn that the present was the only moment there is and that happiness lay in wanting, experiencing, and celebrating what they already had, rather than in trying to get what they thought they wanted.

Those who participated in these movements were typically from the more comfortable sectors of Western societies, from social groups which had benefited from above-average education and incomes. The working classes and ethnic minorities were absent from the new religions. Cost no doubt had something to do with it—an Exegesis weekend cost £200 at 1984 prices; an est weekend $400—but skilled manual workers could have afforded those prices had they been interested. To understand their lack of interest we need to look more closely at the problem which world-affirming new religious movements claimed to solve.

In an achievement-oriented society, success may have a high price in self-control, the postponement of gratification, and the repression of instinctual desires. A participant in an Actualizations training seminar said:

All my life, I've been an achiever. I've always won all of the 'Best of Everything' awards. I've been rising fast in the corporation I work for, looking forward—somewhat uneasily—to the day when they make me president of the company. It's a goal I have absolutely no doubt that I'll achieve. There's just one drawback. I feel the closer I get, the less human I am. It's robbing me of my humanity.[13]

While they have become comfortable in material terms, some people may feel that they have done so at the price of repressing their 'real' selves, creating a strait-jacket around their expressive desires, and placing barriers between themselves and their loved ones. Thus there arises a demand—met by some of the world-affirming new religions—

for a context and method for liberating spontaneity, for contacting the real self behind the masks and the performances, and for feeling and sharing intimacy and love, if only for a weekend, before the return to the impersonal realities of urban industrial life.

However, it is not just the human problems which world-affirming new religions aim to solve which point to a middle-class market. There are also entry qualifications. I will return to this shortly, but it seems clear that to feel at home among Rajneesh's Neo-Sannyasins and the students of est requires a degree of self-regard and self-confidence. It is a lot easier to imagine that, appropriately adjusted, the self is a powerful autonomous agent if your work offers autonomy and some opportunity for creativity than if you are part of a large semi-skilled manual labour force and pressingly aware of how little you can affect anything.

There is a further sense in which the world-affirming new religions are a product of the rationalization of the modern world and that is in their view of the self as an appropriate site for remedial action. The US sociologist Peter Berger and his associates have argued that, in addition to the obvious material and social consequences of technology, modern technological work inevitably brings with it a new kind of consciousness. This new way of thinking has its most immediate impact in the world of work and the economy (for example, in leading managements to model relations between personnel on the form of a production-line process) but it spreads so that it colours even those spheres which were thought to provide 'rest and recreation' for a soul dehumanized by the world of work. We see the rational industrial commitment to improving productivity and efficiency in our remedial approach to our bodies and our personalities. We are no longer expected to be 'ourselves'. Indeed, we have a duty to discover our 'real' selves by working at it. This is one of the paradoxes of naturalism. We are supposed to 'just be yourself' but we attain that authentic state by working hard to change into the sort of person the instructor or therapist or 'resource person' thinks we ought to be. Relationships have to be 'worked at'. A room of middle-class people talking about their childhoods is a 'workshop'. The publishers of those monthly magazines—'Buy Part 1 and get Part 2 free!'—that build into a comprehensive library of instruction for gardening, home decorating, or car repair now offer manuals for improving fitness, beauty, and personal relationships.

But notice the point of such work and attention. Unlike the disciplines of the medieval monk or the 'method' of the Methodists, these modern techniques are not designed to help us conform to an external ethical code and better to glorify God. They are designed to make us happy: to allow us to fulfil our human potential. As Philip Rieff puts it: 'a sense of well-being has become the end, rather than a by-product of striving after some superior communal end.'[14]

What sort of people are attracted to the New Age? First, like the new religions of the 1970s, the New Age is popular in the most affluent and cosmopolitan parts of the country. A lot of New Age activity is found in the south-east of England, and the centres in places like the north of Scotland, the English Lake District, and Wales have been founded by New Agers from London and the home counties who have moved to the sparsely populated edges in order to get back to nature and to acquire cheap property which can be used to generate income through hosting workshops and residential conferences. The Findhorn Foundation in Moray attracts its members and visitors from the home counties and the metropolitan centres of Europe; it has very few recruits from Moray. Secondly, and this is related to the first observation, there are precious few working-class New Agers. Spiritual growth appeals mainly to those people whose more pressing material needs have been satisfied. Unmarried mothers raising children on welfare tend to be too concerned with finding food, heat, and light to be overly troubled by their inner lights, and when they do look for release from their troubles they prefer the bright outer lights of bars and discothèques. That many of the virtuosi New Agers sacrificed middle-class standards of living to embark on their voyages of self-discovery does not change the fact that their preference for spiritual satisfaction over material satisfaction has very little appeal to those who have yet to enjoy the latter. There is all the difference in the world between the sectarian 'religions of the oppressed' that allow whole groups of people to make sense of their deprivations by turning them into marks of grace and the occasionally ascetic spirituality of the well off who like a little self-denial for their soul's sake. We can be slightly more specific and expect that the spiritual dynamics of the New Age will most appeal to the university-educated middle classes working in the 'expressive professions': social workers, counsellors, actors, writers, artists, and others whose education and work cause them to have an articulate interest in human potential.

Though we can imagine how the promise of esoteric knowledge and power might appeal to the socially and personally inadequate, the occult does not seem disproportionately to attract people with major personality disorders. To see the attraction of the New Age as *compensation* for what is missing in someone's life is to overlook important points about self-confidence and the created nature of needs. With its interest in the 'self' and its fondness for the encounter group, the human-growth part of the New Age appeals primarily to those who have the vocabulary and the confidence to think and talk about their 'selves'. Furthermore, and I want to stress this because it is central to the bigger issue of secularization, the explanation I gave above of the appeal of the new religions needs to be carefully restated so that the complex relationship between predispositions, needs, and rewards is correctly understood.

It is a mistake to suppose that we have needs which drive us to this or that activity so that we can read backwards from the rewards that the new activity provides and see their absence in the earlier state as the *cause* of our involvement. Needs are not fixed things which demand their satisfaction. In common with other primates, we have a few fundamental needs, but how we conceive of these and attempt to satisfy them is a product of our socialization into a particular culture. We all need food, but we cannot explain why the French eat horses by saying that they are hungry. We may all have a basic instinct for sexual expression, but many cultures have lauded celibacy and there is such a range of ways of sexual expression that there is nothing we can imagine that is not commonplace in some culture. Cultural innovations are not explained simply by showing the roots of the needs they satisfy. We can observe as a matter of fact that success in middle-class careers is often bought at the price of deferring gratification and repressing desires for so long that the ability for guilt-free enjoyment and spontaneity is lost, but this of itself does not mean that people in that position will see it like that. They may be only vaguely aware that they are dissatisfied until the cultural innovation comes along which simultaneously asserts that they have a problem, that the problem is of this nature, and that this idea or therapy is a cure for the condition. That is, a perception of the problem and the solution *interact* with each other.

There is an important reason for labouring this rather abstract point. Religions offer explanations for practical problems (why is the Black Death killing my family?) and answers to metaphysical questions (what is the chief end of man?). As already noted, some scholars conclude from the universal nature of such problems and questions that there is a persistent human need for religion and hence that secularization can only be temporary. I am suggesting a very different understanding of the human condition. Practical problems and existential questions do not come like Paddington Bear with labels round their necks telling us what they mean. They need to be interpreted and interpretation is a matter of culture. In a religious culture people will frame their questions in religious terms and hence will seek religious answers. In a secular culture the same problems will be interpreted very differently. Few of us take AIDS to be a divine judgement. Horrific as were the death-rates of the First World War, they did not trigger a religious revival in Britain because by then few people were disposed to think in religious terms.

To return to the specific issue of the appeal of the New Age, the social characteristics that predispose some people to take it seriously are better thought of, not as pre-existing deficiencies which the innovation remedies, but as conditions for finding the innovation plausible. People with no prior experience of introverted self-inspection, no fluency in the language of self-examination, and no confidence in self-expression find New Age spirituality incomprehensible and hence will not interpret their problems in ways which the New Age addresses.

Like the traditional churches, the New Age appeals more to women than to men. Women have long held founding and leading roles in deviant religious movements, especially those that stress charisma and spirit possession. One could mention the twelfth-century mystic Hildegard of Bingen or the fourteenth-century Dame Julian of Norwich. From the nineteenth century one could cite Madame Blavatsky and Annie Besant, two of the founders of Theosophy, Ellen White of the Seventh Day Adventists, Mary Baker-Eddy of Christian Science, or Ann Lee, who founded the Shakers. The first seances of modern spiritualism were conducted by the Fox sisters. It is a rough-and-ready picture, but in terms of gender, the New Age divides. The parapsychology and esoteric knowledge side tends to be male; the healing, channelling, and spirituality side tends to be female. My own count of 500 people entering the hall for the Mind, Body, and Spirit convention in 1993 gave a female-to-male ratio of about 2 to 1.

Why women should be more interested in matters spiritual than men is clearly an enormous subject and I can only sketch an answer by drawing attention to two general areas. First, there is the *focus* of religious activity. The churches have always been interested in the control of sexuality and in the instruction of the next generation, both matters which are concentrated on the domestic hearth and in which women have a major role to play. With secularization and the withdrawal of the churches from public and political life, religion becomes increasingly concerned with the domestic world, the sphere in which women are traditionally socialized to give a lead. To return to the simplified division of the social world to which I have referred a number of times in this book, the modern divide between the private world and the public world, with religion relegated to the former, increases its relevance for women and diminishes it for men.

But as well as there being an obvious resonance between spirituality and the traditional roles of women, there is also an affinity with widely held conceptions of femininity. Some feminists argue that there are no significant differences between men and women which are not the product of gender socialization (and hence which cannot be changed), but more common is the claim that women are essentially if not enormously different from (and superior to) men because their child-bearing and rearing experiences make them less confrontational, less aggressive, less goal oriented, less domineering, more co-operative, and more caring. Where men wish to achieve, women wish to feel. This would certainly fit with the expressive emphasis of the New Age as much as with more traditional religions.

There is also a crucial point about roles *per se*. As I have already noted, the New Age rests on the premiss that the self is basically good and that problems stem from its being confined by institutional roles. In that sense, the New Age critique of gender roles is more far-reaching than that of much feminist literature. It is not only the present patriarchal roles which need to be challenged. Rather it is the whole practice of encouraging people to interact on the basis of roles which must be replaced by authenticity. Although there are 'new men' who are attracted to the idea of changing gender roles, it is clear that any restructuring will have greater appeal to the group most likely to benefit from the change—that is, to women.

The observation about gender needs to be tied to that about class. In so far as working-class women outside the churches are interested in the supernatural, it tends to be in its older forms: fortune-telling, horoscopes, superstitions, and charms. They see themselves as passive, pushed by obscure forces beyond their control and almost beyond their ken. They do not see themselves as empowered nor the 'self' as having the potential which the New Age assigns it.

The Significance of the New Age

As with my earlier comments of the new religious movements of the 1970s, the first point to be made about the social significance of the New Age is that the numbers of those intimately involved in it, the *habitués* of the cultic milieu, are few.

The counter-cultural end of the New Age is certainly sparsely populated. Though at its height Findhorn attracted hundreds of young people, most stayed for short periods. Even if the number who have stayed or any length of time reached 10,000 (and it might be some way short of that), this would be less than the membership of Ian Paisley's Free Presbyterian Church of Ulster and far less than the number of people lost to the Christian churches in Scotland in a decade. The more mainstream human-potential organizations will have influenced more people. Heelas estimates that, in the final year of its operations (which ran from 1977 to 1984), Exegesis trained more than 6,000 people. Insight claims over 100,000 participants world-wide since 1978. Between 1977 and 1984, about 8,000 people in Britain took est training courses. If one takes together a variety of est-like programmes, perhaps 50,000 people have been involved. On top of that we would expect a considerable 'multiplier'. It is in the very nature of cultic involvement that people acquire expertise and then pass on what they have learnt (or a diluted or mixed version of what they have learnt) to their partners and friends. But there is an obvious trade-off between numbers and impact. For many consumers, New Age ideas and therapies are leisure pursuits, foreign holidays for the self. Some of us go hiking; others spend a fortnight at Findhorn. Some of us read crime novels; others read books about the Tarot. It is clear that, whatever it does for how those involved feel and think about the world, the New Age has far fewer behavioural consequences than sectarian religion.

There is little or no impact on the world at large. The state, civic society, the polity, and the economy remain unaffected. In so far as any New Age interests have achieved some impact, it has been because they have coincided with more powerful and mundane forces. If Western European governments are now interested in ecology, it is because of self-interest rather than respect for a super-organism called Gaia.

The low impact and low salience of the New Age are not an accident. Taken narrowly, the influence of the New Age is bound to be small because its individualism prevents it having a cumulative effect. New Age channelling differs from Victorian spiritualism in one regard which clearly shows its affinity with the culture of the modern world: it is more democratic. In Christian or Muslim mysticism there is one God out there and only some of us are sufficiently spiritual to hear him. In Victorian and Edwardian spiritualism there is a world of spirits out there and very few of us are sufficiently receptive to hear them. But in the New Age, as in the most radical forms of Quakerism, the God is within and all of us have the potential to tune in to ourselves. The near-universal availability of divine knowledge means that any strand of the New Age must inevitably be organized as a cult rather than as a sect. Even those purveyors of a particular piece of esoteric knowledge who wish to recruit a committed and enduring following have little choice but to recognize the operating principle of the New Age milieu, which is one of almost complete acceptance of alternative views. The denominational forms of Christianity are at least given a degree of cohesion by their shared histories, traditional liturgies, and common language. In the cultic world of the New Age there is no binding tradition—only an individualistic gutting of a rich variety of traditions.

Each individual chooses which claims to expertise to recognize, and the fact that the revelation is being paid for strengthens the hand of the consumer. Instead of the enduring obligation to follow a leader found in charismatic religious movements, we see the limited contract of buyer and seller. Having paid to attend the workshop or to buy the book, the purchaser decides the extent and nature of his or her commitment. With everyone paying the piper, everyone calls his or her own tune.

The consequences of radical individualism for various aspects of the New Age are worth pursuing. First, it is clear that 'new science' will always be incapable of coming anywhere near to matching 'old' science because, though arguments can be handled by the posture of relativism (everything is true), they cannot be resolved in specific detail and hence knowledge cannot advance. The individualism of New Age thought prevents any testing of Alper's claims about the crystal power of Atlantis against competing or modified stories. Anyone can add or subtract from Alper's revelation, and there are no rational grounds for knowing what additions or subtractions make the new version more or less accurate than the original.

Secondly, New Age individualism inhibits the development of a body of shared values beyond those which allow individualism. Anyone who attends a large number of New Age seminars, listens to a large number of cassettes, or reads sufficient issues of *One World* or *Kindred Spirit* gets the impression that certain revelations would be unacceptable. It is hard to imagine (though doubtless such things are there on the fringes) that many channellings will support racism, sexism, hierarchy, authoritarianism, cruelty to animals, or the despoilation of the environment, but, were New Agers given to argument, even these limits would be contestable. The limited-value consensus of the New Age reflects the value consensus of the culture from which its adherents are drawn, but it gives little guidance as to which new revelations of esoteric knowledge to accept or, in terms of behaviour, how to conduct oneself in any particular setting.

The fallibility of the inner light is abundantly illustrated by the failure of leading New Agers to order their lives any better than the rest of us. The emotional and sexual lives of the founders of Findhorn were by anyone's standards a mess. Eileen Caddy left her first husband and five children to run off with Peter Caddy only to be periodically abandoned by him to the malign influence of his first wife Sheena, who abused and dominated Eileen and even abducted Eileen's first child by Peter. Peter, a handsome, glamorous, and powerful figure, had affairs with many of the young idealistic women who visited the community and he eventually left his wife for a Californian. In all he married five times. One obituarist tried to find a silver lining in what others might reasonably view as a history of failure by noting that each change of partner 'coincided with a major change of direction'.[15] Talk of loving everyone masks the more commonplace reality that New Age personal relationships are as or more messy than the entanglements of those of us who are not in tune with our divine selves or the cosmic consciousness. With no comprehensive and binding ethical code, in the New Age there is always the danger that pursuing self-growth actually means pursuing self-interest.

To put it simply, radical individualism prevents the formation of a powerful and influential movement on the lines of, for example, Methodism. The TM promise of the collective power of meditators being greater than the sum of the individuals is false: the New Age has specific effects smaller than the sum of its interested parties because the inherent relativism reduces the conviction and certainty with which any individual consumer holds and lives out his or her esoteric knowledge.

If, in contrast to the church and sect forms of religion, the cultic milieu of the New Age has little effect in radically changing the lives of most of its *habitués* (and hence even less effect on those outside it), it may none the less be of great significance as an expression, and further cause, of a major cultural shift. The New Age exemplifies in stark relief assumptions which in dilute form are widespread and which, because they are not accidental, point us to central features of modernity.

Though its specific cosmologies and mechanics have not become popular, the 'holism' of new science has become widely accepted at least as a rhetorical device. We now have 'Well Woman' clinics which at least pay lip service to the idea that a person's health should be looked at *in toto* and in its personal and social context and not be viewed as a set of unconnected problems to be managed separately. Our respect for the enormous accomplishments of modern science and medicine (a man on the moon and a simultaneous five-organ transplant) are tempered by fears of that power to intervene (Chernobyl and the Thalidomide babies). The contrast between the natural and the technological is well established with a strong preference for the former (where it can be adopted without losing the benefits of the latter). We will not do without our freezers, personal computers, and mobile phones, but we will purchase a quite implausible range of consumer products that are advertised as 'natural', 'traditional', and 'country style'. Pharmacists sell homoeopathic remedies. Even quite esoteric therapies have been incorporated in the product ranges of conventional capitalist enterprises. The Body Shop, a soap and cosmetics company that has created a highly successful international corporation on the appeal of its politically correct 'natural' products and minimalist packaging, in 1992 adopted aromatherapy and marketed a range of 'essential oils'. A year later, Marks and Spencer PLC, the epitome of the solid respectable quality supermarket, followed suit with its range of aromatherapy bubble bath liquids.

Just as TM successfully took the Hinduism out of yoga, the Body Shop has taken the esoteric out of essential oils. Further to reduce the already minimal change in life-style demanded by these consumerist versions of the original practices, the Body Shop suggests meditating while wearing the aromatherapy mask, thus saving twenty minutes!

Good Housekeeping, the most staid of women's magazines, has published a directory of 'Complementary Health' which, with no critical or

---

AROMATHERAPY THE BODY SHOP WAY

To clear away much of the mysticism and doubt that surrounds aromatherapy, we've put together our own range that anybody can enjoy, regardless of age, sex or way of life. We want to make it as easy as possible for people to find out just how good aromatherapy can make them feel.

There's nothing complicated about our range and you don't need any specialist knowledge to use it. Here's how easy it is—when you're soaking in a relaxing bath, why not treat your face to an aromatherapy mask? Or skip a cup of coffee in the morning and try showering with our reviving shower oil instead. The uses of aromatherapy are endless. Build it into your daily routine and you'll soon reap the benefits!

We can make you feel good!

To make it easy to decide which aromatherapy products will suit you, we've divided our range into relaxing (red packaging) and reviving (blue packaging).

Source: The Body Shop, 'Aromatherapy' (1992).

evaluative comment, happily lists, among others, 'Crystal Therapy' ('for example, amber is meant to help digestive problems and malachite to cure inflammation') and 'Polarity Therapy' ('based on the theory that your chakras, or central energy sources, are neutral and that all points beyond them are positive or negative. . . . Illness occurs when the flow of energy through the body is slowed down or blocked. When this happens practitioners will place their hands on the body . . . to correct the balance and flow of energy').[16] And it is this lack of judgement which is significant about the mainstreaming of the New Age. Where once such respectable and popular leaders of opinion and disseminators of information as major periodicals, the electronic media, and educational institutions would have felt a responsibility critically to evaluate cultural innovations, now they simply present them all in a cafeteria counter and allow the consumers to make their own choices, not only about what is good or moral but also about what cures ailments and explains the nature of the universe.

This is the importance of the New Age. It illustrates the zenith of individualism. Individualism used to mean the right to act as one wished provided it did not harm others and the right to hold views radically at odds with the consensus. It has now shifted up in abstraction from a behavioural and ethical principle to an epistemological claim. It is now asserted as the right to decide what is and is not true. This conclusion no doubt exaggerates slightly, but it will be stated boldly so that its import is readily grasped. What the New Age shows us is that a steady increase in spending on formal education has been accompanied by a decline in faith in the possibility of authoritative knowledge. The egalitarianism and democracy of modern societies pose a basic threat to the science and knowledge base of those societies. Amplified by widespread literacy and extremely cheap ways of communicating ideas, the egalitarian ethos presents a huge array of incompatible and conflicting ideas at the same time as it encourages a large number of people to believe that they have as great an insight into the workings of the world as anyone else. The inevitable consequence is relativism, not just in matters of behaviour—we have long passed the point of being able to agree on how we should behave—but now in the realms of knowledge. The judgements of any groups of experts can be dismissed with a flippant assertion of partiality: 'they would say that, wouldn't they?' Any layman who can read can claim to understand the origins of the world or the causes of depression.

When the very idea of authoritative knowledge is under attack in such spheres as science and medicine, where it seems so obvious that there is a vast gulf between the expert and the lay person, how much more difficult is it to sustain the notion of authority in the sphere of religion?

Further Reading

In addition to the vast body of promotional and critical work, there is a considerable sociological literature on new religious movements. Two very good introductions are Eileen Barker, *New Religious Movements: A Practical Introduction* (London: HMSO, 1989), and Roy Wallis, *The Elementary Forms of the New Religious Life* (London: Routledge & Kegan Paul, 1984). The following are excellent examples of detailed case studies: Eileen Barker, *The Making of a Moonie: Choice or Brainwashing* (Oxford: Blackwell, 1984); Roy Wallis, *The Road to Total Freedom: A Sociological Analysis of Scientology* (London: Heinemann, 1976); Bryan Wilson and Karel Dobbelaere, *A Time to Chant: The Soka Gakkai Buddhists in Britain* (Oxford: Oxford University Press, 1994); Steven M. Tipton, *Getting Saved From the Sixties: Moral Meaning in Conversion and Cultural Change* (Berkeley: University of California Press, 1982).

William Bloom, *The New Age* (London: Rider, 1991), is a well-chosen anthology of New Age writings. An invaluable reference book is J. Gordon Melton, Jerome Clark, and Aidan A. Kelly, *New Age Almanac* (New York: Visible Ink, 1991). For insider's accounts, see Eileen Caddy and Liza Hollingshead, *Flight into Freedom: The Autobiography of the Co-Founder of the Findhorn Community* (Longmead, Dorset: Element Books, 1988); Carol Riddell, *The Findhorn Community: Creating a Human Identity for the 21st Century* (Findhorn, Forres, Moray: Findhorn Press, 1990); and Judith L. Boice, *At One With All Life: A Personal Journal in Gaian Communities* (Findhorn, Forres, Moray: Findhorn Press, 1989).

The best recent ethnography of any part of the New Age is T. M. Luhrman, *Persuasions of the Witch's Craft: Ritual Magic in Contemporary England* (Oxford: Blackwell, 1989). For an insightful and well-referenced social-science study of the general phenomenon, see Paul Heelas, *The New Age: Celebrating the Self* (Oxford: Blackwell, forthcoming).

For a general introduction to the sociological understanding of modernity and for specific insights into the place of religion in the modern world, see the following works of Peter Berger and his associates; Peter L. Berger and Thomas Luckmann, *The Social Construction of Reality* (London: Allen Lane, 1967); Peter L. Berger, *The Social Reality of*

Religion (London: Faber and Faber, 1967) (published in the United States as *The Sacred Canopy*); and Peter L. Berger, Brigitte Berger, and Hansfried Kellner, *The Homeless Mind: Modernization and Consciousness* (New York: Vintage Books, 1974).

Chapter Five

The Big Picture

Although international comparisons have not been made explicit, at many points in the previous chapters I have implied that the patterns and trends we see in the religious life of modern Britain are not unique. In this conclusion I want to draw the themes presented above into a comprehensive explanation of *secularization*, which I take to be a central characteristic of modern industrial societies.

There is very widespread agreement that Britain's religious life is not what it used to be. Although not regarded with any great hostility, our churches are unpopular, their teachings are ignored by the vast majority of the population, their leaders no longer have the ears of our rulers, their efforts to glorify God are barely noticed, and their beliefs no longer inform the presuppositions of the wider culture. Within the churches, much of the specific belief content of Christianity has been allowed to disappear from sight or has been radically rewritten to make it accord with rational and secular thought. Many of those who continue to attend to the supernatural are oriented, not to an external God and his writ over the world and all that it contains, but to the inner self. There are enclaves where religion remains potent—where it is closely associated with a threatened ethnic identity, where its adherents have isolated themselves from the mainstream, and where it aids ethnic minorities in coming to terms with their place in a new world—but they are only enclaves. In so far as the supernatural or the spiritual is still to be found in the mainstream, it is in almost homoeopathic concentrations: so watered down as to be a shadow of its former self, nearly undetectable to the untrained eye.

We must, of course, be careful that this general image of modern Britain as a secular society does not so colour our vision that we are blind to the presence of religion today or exaggerate how religious were our forebears. Not every ploughman who homeward plodded his weary way was a true believer and not every Essex stockbroker is an atheist. None the less, the general direction of change is unmistakable.

This does not mean that the secularization thesis, as it is about to be summarized, is universally accepted. If for no other reason, the need for scholars of every new generation to make their names by overturning the orthodoxies of their predecessors would ensure that my account would have its critics, and they are many, although it is worth noting that they are almost all sociologists of religion. Students of other disciplines and other areas of sociology clearly do not believe that religion is an important social fact to which they must attend. Alternatives to my account of religious change are cited in the Further Reading section for this chapter, and there is no scope here to address any but the most general or most wayward criticisms.

It is often asserted that the secularization approach assumes that religion has declined as, and because, people got smarter. Truth displaced falsehood. Certainly one finds committed atheists—the sort of people who join Rationalist and Humanist associations—and some very liberal Christians arguing that religion has lost its medieval dominance because modern people are too clever to believe in old superstitions. Some influential early social scientists held similar views. The nineteenth-century Frenchman Auguste Comte believed that the new science of sociology would replace the old myths. Sigmund Freud declared his hand when he called one of his books on religion *The Future of an Illusion*. Karl Marx expected socialism to make redundant what he regarded as the 'opiate of the masses'. But no modern account of secularization assumes that we (or our culture) are superior to what went before or that religion has declined because it is false. The history of the human ability to believe very strongly in what turns out to be nonsense suggests that whether something is true or false and whether or not it becomes widely accepted are two very different questions. Whether religion or any particular religion is true is a theological, not a sociological, question. Fortunately we can avoid such unprofitable terrain by recognizing that all beliefs—true ones as much as false ones—need explaining. Hence we can ask what is it about our societies, other than the supposed greater maturity of modern people, that explains why religious beliefs are less plausible or credible than once they were.

A second common criticism is that the secularization approach assumes the decline in the social significance of religion to be uniform, regular, and irreversible, and hence that it is refuted by evidence of religious revivals or continued religiosity in modern society. Such criticism misunderstands the nature of explanation in the social sciences. Modern societies are not homogeneous, like jars of food for babies aged 3–7 months. They are lumpy, and in identifying general trends we are talking about probabilities and percentages, not making invariant and universal claims. We also need to remember that, unlike the objects whose reactions are explained by the laws of natural science, we are dealing with conscious sentient beings who can respond to the trends the sociologist identifies by trying to subvert the predictions.

A third criticism of the claim that modernity undermines the plausibility of the supernatural is that it is refuted by such contemporary revivals of politicized religious fervour as we see in Iran or Pakistan or the Punjab. Again, this simply misunderstands what is being asserted. As will be clear, 'modern' here does not mean 'extant in our time'; it means possessing most or all of the features listed below. The Kalahari bushmen are still about, but no one would cite their culture as relevant to arguments about the effects of modernization.

This clarification does raise another objection to using modernization as the 'cause' of secularization. There is always a danger in showing the close connections of the two processes that one might actually define them in such a way that they are the same. Then, instead of a causal claim along the lines of 'vegetarian pasties make me sick', we have only a tautology, a proposition that is true only because the second part is merely a restatement of the first: 'all triangles have three sides' is a good example. However, I hope that the way I have formulated the relationship between modernization and the decline of religion clearly distinguishes the two processes.

Enough of the preliminaries; what explains secularization? A cursory glance at countries and social groups within countries which are least religious suggests that it has something to do with modernization. By modernization I mean the whole package of economic, political, cultural, and social changes that come with increasing reliance on inanimate rather than animate sources of power. The Egyptians built the pyramids with men and beasts; we build with machines and carbon fuels. Clearly modernization, like secularization, is a multi-faceted process and we cannot expect that, in every example, every facet will be identical, but then life is complicated!

The Social Consequences of Modernization

One obvious feature of modernization is the division of single social institutions into smaller but more specialized units. The family was once a unit of economic production as well as the site for biological and cultural reproduction. George Eliott's Silas Marner wove his cloth while looking after his foundling daughter, and he did both at home. Now we go out to work. The family was once the site for all education and socialization. Now we have special places called schools to which people go to be educated by professional educators.

Ideas from the world of production and exchange—the need to increase efficiency, supply, and demand as the fixer of price, and so on—are so powerful in our culture that it is difficult to believe that the medieval church made a valiant attempt to control such matters. In the fourteenth century, lending money for profit was regarded as sinful and the Church's own courts claimed jurisdiction over usurers. A century before, craft guilds used church courts to enforce their restrictive practices and to try breaches of contract. Modernization sees the freeing of economic activity from religiously sanctioned controls and the development of the world of work as an autonomous sphere driven only by its own values. Gradually other aspects of life go the same way. Education, social welfare, health care, and social control have mostly passed out of church control, and where churches still run such activities they do so in ways that differ little from the secular provision.

At the same time, as life becomes divided into evermore specialized areas, so the people become divided into distinct classes and social groups. Economic growth leads to the emergence of an ever greater range of occupation and life-situation. Although there were considerable disparities of wealth in feudal societies, most people lived similar lives and they lived cheek-by-jowl. In medieval tower houses and castles, the gentry and their servants often slept in the same room, separated only by curtains. They ate at the same table, with the salt dish marking the gentry from the riff-raff. Because there was a strong hierarchical social structure which was quite open and clear about differences in status, superiors did not feel threatened by the presence of their minions and could inhabit the same physical and mental space. As classes developed, especially with the shift to the cities with the growth of big factories, people spent more and more of their time only with others in the same economic circumstances and less and less time with their superiors or subordinates.

This separating-out has been hastened by the rise of egalitarianism discussed briefly in Chapter One. Innovation and economic expansion have brought with them occupational mobility. People no longer do the job they have always done because their family has always done that job. Occupational change makes it hard for people to internalize visions of themselves that suppose permanent inferiority. They cannot be improving themselves and their class position while thinking that they have a fixed 'station' or 'degree' in a hierarchical world. Modern societies are thus inherently egalitarian.

Furthermore, economic expansion brings contact with strangers. Profound inequalities of status would only be tolerable and not lead to constant friction if the hierarchy was widely known and accepted. Soldiers can move from one regiment to another and still know their place because there is a uniform (in both senses) ranking system. In a complex and interacting mobile society, there is no way of ensuring that we know whether we are superior or subordinate to this new person. Once people have trouble knowing who should bow first, they give up bowing and basic equality becomes the normal presumption.

Thirdly, the separation of work and home, of the public and the private, makes for equality. One cannot be a serf from sunrise to sunset and then an autonomous individual for the evening and at weekends. A real serf has to be full time. A temporary work-role is not a full identity, and, though work-roles are usually part of a hierarchy, they can no longer structure the whole world-view. In the absence of a shared belief system which would sanction inequality and subjection (and the decline of religion usually removes that), egalitarianism becomes the default position.

Democracy was slow to come, but the creation of a modern economy brought with it the general interactional presumption that we are 'much of a muchness'. It was ironic that this exaggerated rather than diminished social distance. The better off, now a little unsure about the legitimacy of their superiority, moved to safeguard their prerogatives by physically moving away from the poor. As towns and cities developed, they did so with clear class divisions. About 1775 the Edinburgh bourgeoisie began to abandon the old town, where judges and poor artisans had inhabited flats (of very different quality) in the same tenement building, for the social exclusiveness of the New Town. As the public world became more clearly separated from the private and came to be informed by egalitarianism, those rich enough used their privacy to divide themselves from the rest. Different social groups began to see the world in different ways. The idea of a single moral universe in which all manner and condition of persons have a place in some single grand design became less and less plausible.

Here, as at every stage of the process, the religious culture informs the social changes. Where (as in Catholic countries) religion is legitimated by a single authoritative source and people are faced with the stark choice between accepting or rejecting that authority, the fragmentation of the society creates a single fault line and the society splits between those who continue to support the Church and an anti-clerical bloc which seeks to destroy it. Hence it is in Catholic France, Spain, Portugal, and Italy that there are a powerful church and a powerful Communist movement. The Protestant tradition which came to dominate British Christianity, by rejecting an external authority, made it possible for different groups to rework the gospel in ways suited to their changing circumstances. Instead of one great split, the religious culture fragments, like a car windscreen, into small pieces. Opposition to the privileges of the church that supports the privileged can be expressed in competing sects and need not produce aggressive anti-clericalism.

The general fragmentation of community and social life is accompanied by what Bryan Wilson has called 'societalization', the process by which 'life is increasingly enmeshed and organized, not locally but societally (that society being most evidently, but not uniquely, the nation state)'.[1] Close-knit, integrated, small-scale communities have disappeared, undermined and replaced by large-scale industrial and commercial enterprise; by the emergence of modern nation-states co-ordinated through massive, impersonal bureaucracies; and by the development of anonymous urban agglomerations as the typical residential setting. The decline of community damages religion in three ways. When every birth, marriage, and death in generation after generation was celebrated and marked with the same rituals in the same building, then the religion that legitimated those rituals was powerful and persuasive because it was woven into the life of the village. When the total, all-embracing community, working and playing together, gives way to the dormitory town or suburb, there is little held in common left to celebrate.

Secondly, when the shift from community to society (typically a nation-state) is accompanied by the fragmentation of the religious culture, churches are simply not able to retain a broad range of social functions. Both fairness and efficiency require that the priest, pastor, and minister be replaced by the secular professional, church-based provision by secular national services.

The decline of community not only deprives churches of things to do; it also fundamentally changes the way in which religious beliefs are held. Beliefs are strongest when they are unexamined and naïvely accepted as the way things are; when they form part of what phenomenologists call the 'taken-for-granted' world. And that condition is most easily achieved when the particular world-view is uncritically shared by the entire social group in which one lives and moves and is constantly reinforced by every little element of social interaction. Modern societies are culturally diverse places that no longer offer such constant background reaffirmation of any particular world-view. Especially when it is embodied in democratic political structures, basic egalitarianism prevents even a large and élite minority imposing its vision on the rest of society. What appears at first as a practical freedom—we can worship at any altar or none—has profound consequences for the way we can think about that worship. Religious belief is now obviously a matter of choice. We may still choose to believe, but we cannot easily hide from ourselves the knowledge that we choose God rather than God choosing us. God may still be respected and loved but that he no longer need be feared means that one major source of motivation for getting religion right and making sure that your children get it right has been removed.

As modernization brings cultural choice, so it also makes it less likely that we will choose to believe in God and less likely that such belief will bear much resemblance to the religious culture of pre-modern societies.

Rationalization

Modernization not only causes a fundamental change in the nature of social relationships; it also causes a major change in how we think about the world. In particular it brings rationality. Though many of us would find aspects of what is meant by that term laudable, it should not in the first instance be confused with virtue or goodness. We mean a concern with the systematic search for the most efficient means to a given end. We believe that the fairest and most efficient way of organizing anything on a large scale is to establish rules and procedures which constrain actions and decisions to the matter in hand, narrowly defined. Having created those procedures, we do not view them as sacred and immutable. If someone can suggest a more efficient means of achieving the same end, we change our methods.

A crucial component of the rational attitude is the assumption of regularity in the world. The sun rises and the sun sets. What worked yesterday will work today, all things being equal, and if it does not, we set about trying to discover what has changed. We live in a world of timetables and calendars that allow us to record appointments for next year. Very few of us expect a sudden invasion of the supernatural. Very conservative Protestant churches still have on their notice boards 'Meeting 11 a.m. (DV)' but that *Deo volente* or 'God willing' is a residue. In practice almost no one expects that God will intervene to prevent the next service taking place.

We can readily see how a world of rationality is less conducive to religion than a traditional society. Everything is seen as potentially improvable. Everything can be made more efficient. We find it very easy to talk about means and procedures but very difficult to discuss transcendental ends. *The Shorter Catechism*, that seventeenth-century distillation of the key points that was used to teach Scottish Presbyterians their faith, has as its first question: 'What is the chief end of man?' In our societies such a question is rarely asked because we know that we cannot agree an answer.

Thus far I have not mentioned science and technology, and that delay has been deliberate. When asked to explain the decline of religion, a lot of people mention the rise of Western science and the competition between scientific explanations and religious ones. They point out that many of the beliefs of the early Christians have been shown to be wrong. The earth is round and not flat. The earth moves round the sun and not the sun around the earth. The earth and human life are vastly older than the ages traditionally taken from biblical accounts. While scientists recognize that there are still huge gaps in our knowledge, there is a consensus that an evolutionary model along the lines of Darwinism offers a better explanation of the origins of species than does the account of divine creation in seven days given in the Old Testament book of Genesis.

For all that, I do not actually think that science has *directly* contributed much to secularization. There are all sorts of ways in which we can insulate our beliefs from apparently contradicting evidence if we want to. We can easily avoid hearing the troublesome evidence. We can dismiss it by blackening the character of those who bring the bad news. However, and this is important for understanding what circumstances allow minority views to be sustained, such strategies must be widely shared. Though the centralizing tendencies of modern nation-states and their mass media tend to erode distinctive visions, a deviant worldview held by enough people is a legitimate cultural preference. The idiosyncratic vision of the single individual is lunacy.

The greatest damage done by science and technology to religious world-views is not in displacing religiously sanctioned ideas about the world (though they have done that) but in subtly altering the way we think about the world so as to make religious beliefs and rituals ever more irrelevant. Again one can talk not of social change having an impact on religious culture but of the two things interacting to hasten both in the same direction. Though there is not space to elaborate the argument, a good case can be made for saying that the monotheistic religion of first Judaism and then Christianity encouraged the development of natural science by removing the all-pervasive and unpredictable deities of a pantheistic world. Jews and Christians believed that God created the earth, but, having done so, he then went into semi-retirement and stayed out of its day-to-day operations. Space was thus created for studying the mechanics of that world. The removal in Protestant cultures of the oppressive authority of the Vatican gave a further encouragement to natural scientists. The Puritan natural philosophers may have intended their studies of the glory of God's creation to increase our appreciation for his handiwork, but the outcome was that we were able to understand how the world worked without any reference to its creator.

Science and technology have given us a notion of cause and effect that makes us look first for the natural causal explanation of an event. When an aeroplane crashes with the loss of many lives, we ask not what moral purpose the event had but what was its natural cause. And, in so far as we keep finding those causes (a loose engine nut, a terrorist bomb), we are subtly discouraged from seeking the moral significance. Our attention is further concentrated on the natural world by the success of technology in delivering the goods. Technically efficient machinery and procedures reduce uncertainty and our need for the supernatural. There is no need for religious rites or spells to protect cattle against ringworm when you can buy a drench which has proved over and over to be an excellent cure for the condition. When people had no idea what caused plague and no way of preventing it, shared rituals of repentance were a popular response. Our knowledge of hygiene and our possession of tetracycline remove a whole series of occasions for a revival of religious commitment.

In modern worlds, religion is most used for those dark recessive areas of human life over which control has not been established by technology: unhappiness, extreme stress, and the like. When we have tried every cure for cancer, we pray. When we have revised for our examinations, we pray. We do not pray instead of studying, and even committed believers suppose that a research programme is more likely than a mass prayer meeting to produce a cure for AIDS. Our notion of the scope of the divine, then, is much smaller than that of pre-industrial man.

To summarize, I am suggesting that the effect of science and technology on the plausibility of religious belief is often misunderstood. The clash of ideas between science and religion is far less significant than the more subtle impact of naturalistic ways of thinking about the world. Science and technology have not made us atheists. Rather the fundamental assumptions that underlie them which we can summarily describe as 'rationality' have made the religious approach to life less relevant. We view the material world as an amoral series of invariant relationships of cause and effect. We treat many objects as readily replaceable components: the radiator from any 1.8 litre Vauxhall Cavalier will fit any other Vauxhall Cavalier. We expect our actions to be infinitely reproducible in specified circumstances: if pressing the key combination 'Alt' and 'F4' closes a Windows computer programme today, it will do so tomorrow. We solve new problems by rationally auditing our present state of knowledge and pursuing research programmes to fill the gaps. People who think like that are not incapable of believing in the supernatural and the divine, but they are, in Max Weber's telling phrase, increasingly 'religiously unmusical'.

Whole books have been devoted to the nature and consequences of modernization, and the brief summary above cannot hope to do justice to the complexity of the topic. In particular, it has had to skate over the difficult issue of which consequences of modernization are accidental and which are inevitable. With that admission, the strongest claim that I can make here is that the history of the Western world suggests that rationalization in its many forms is a necessary consequence of industrial production and poses a series of problems for supernatural religions.

To return to the thread that runs through this book, I believe that the essence of the changes in religious cultures which have accompanied modernization can be neatly expressed in terms of the forms of religion best suited to various types of society. With modernization, the church form which dominated the pre-industrial world became untenable and was challenged first by sects and then by general social pressures which saw both church and sect transform into denominations. If we have to pick one single element of modernization that is central to understanding the nature of modern religion, it would be that which explains the rise of the sect, the tolerance at the heart of the denomination, and the amorphous nature of the cult: individualism.

Like the hominid creature drawn on charts of human evolution, who starts on the left-hand side as a small hunched hairy beast and gradually grows and sheds hair until he turns into the sleek human on the right, modernization has seen the individual grow and stand erect. From a stunted and ill-formed beast, subordinate to his Gods as he was subordinate to his political masters, the individual has risen in confidence, claiming first the right to make choices in ever-expanding spheres of behaviour and now insisting, as we saw in Chapter Four, on the right to define reality and then, because the definitions clash, asserting relativism as the practical attitude. Although at first sight worlds apart, the thinking of the denomination and the cult shares the common feature of relativism.

Here I move from historical analysis to speculation, but it seems clear already that the sovereign consumer of capitalism, if he or she insists not only on the right to choose shoe styles and life-styles but also on the right to determine what counts as authoritative knowledge, poses a fundamental threat to the knowledge base and rationality of modern society. Moral relativism, now to be found as much within as outside Christian denominations, is problem enough. Where shared values no longer ensure that we can rub along together, then the need to co-ordinate action will lead to demands for ever greater external technical control. But of possibly greater moment is the epistemological relativism that lies at the heart of the New Age. We should realize its novelty. The religious deviants of previous ages, though they departed from the consensus in specific claims, none the less contended for what they believed to be *the* truth. Our New Age seekers deny the possibility of any authority beyond the preferences of the individual.

If the progression from church, sect, and denomination to cult is, as I have argued, intimately bound up with wider social processes, then those last two forms perhaps carry a vital message for the future. The clear benefits of individualism—the civility, tolerance, and open-mindedness—may soon be outweighed by its costs. The relativist's claim that we choose our lives, free from social constraint, just as we now choose our Gods, is patently false, but the frequently expressed preference for untutored personal choice over hard-won and tested professional expertise may be more than the fashionable dilettantism of a small coterie. It may be part of a wider cultural shift that challenges the rationality on which the modern world is built.

Further Reading

The secularization thesis is actually less of a thesis and more of a general orientation. More detailed versions of the arguments of this chapter can be found in Steve Bruce, *From Cathedrals to Cults: Religion in the Modern World* (Oxford: Oxford University Press, forthcoming); Roy Wallis and Steve Bruce, 'Secularization: Trends, Data and Theory', *Research in the Social Scientific Study of Religion*, 3 (1991), 1–31; and Steve Bruce (ed.), *Religion and Modernization: Sociologists and Historians Debate the Secularization Thesis* (Oxford: Clarendon Press, 1992). The general approach draws heavily on the work of Max Weber, Peter Berger, Bryan Wilson, and David Martin. There are many collections of Weber's writings available. The best short compilation is Max

Weber, *The Sociology of Religion,* translated by Ephraim Fischoff (London: Methuen, 1965). For the others, see Peter L. Berger, *The Social Reality of Religion: Elements of a Sociological Theory of Religion* (London: Faber and Faber, 1969; published in the United States as *The Sacred Canopy*); Bryan Wilson, *Religion in Sociological Perspective* (Oxford: Oxford University Press, 1982), and *Contemporary Transformations of Religion* (Oxford: Oxford University Press, 1976); and David Martin, *A General Theory of Secularization* (Oxford: Blackwell, 1976).

One of the most trenchant critics of the secularization approach in recent years is Rodney Stark. For his alternative, see Rodney Stark and William Sims Bainbridge, *The Future of Religion: Secularisation, Revival and Cult Formation* (Berkeley and Los Angeles: University of California Press, 1985), and *A Theory of Religion* (New York: Peter Lang, 1987); and Roger Finke and Rodney Stark, *The Churching of America 1776–1990: Winners and Losers in our Religious Economy* (New Brunswick, NJ: Rutgers University Press, 1992). For other criticisms, see the various contributions to Bruce (ed.), *Religion and Modernization.*

Notes

Notes to Chapter One

1. For these and many other examples, see Keith Thomas, *Religion and the Decline of Magic* (Harmondsworth, Middx.: Penguin, 1973), 29–56.
2. Rosalind Hill, 'From the Conquest to the Black Death', in Sheridan Gilley and W. J. Sheils (eds.), *A History of Religion in Britain: Practice and Belief from Pre-Roman Times to the Present* (Oxford: Blackwell, 1994), 58.
3. Steve Bruce, *Pray TV: Televangelism in America* (London: Routledge, 1990), 84.

Notes to Chapter Two

1. Richard Hoggart, *The Uses of Literacy* (Harmondsworth, Middx.: Penguin, 1962), 113.
2. It is not easy to draw a single reliable figure for church attendance from the 1851 census. Especially for Scotland, where the returns were less complete than for England and Wales, there are doubts about the reliability of the original figures. There are also problems of interpretation which result from the census counting attendances rather than attenders; many people attended more than one service on a Sunday. Some scholars add morning, afternoon, and evening attendances and make the point that the disappearance of multiple attendance is itself a significant mark of declining commitment and thus should be noted. Others take only the figures for the best attended service, whichever that was for any particular congregation. There is also the issue of whether one follows Horace Mann and leaves in Sunday school scholars. These problems explain why one gets very different reports, even from the same commentator. For example, in his *The Social History of Religion in Scotland since 1730* (London: Methuen, 1987), 19–20, Callum Brown reports 'attendances at church to represent 60.7 per cent of Scottish population and 58.1 per cent of English and Welsh population' but in his *The People in the Pews: Religion and Society in Scotland since 1780* (Glasgow: Economic and Social History Society of Scotland, 1993), 7, he says 'the figure was in the region of 30–35 per cent'! However, we can be confident that, however one seeks to make the 1851 figures comparable to the more recent data, they will be markedly higher than the present rates. I have pooled the estimates of various commentators to produce the estimates in Figure 2.2.
3. Hoggart, *The Uses of Literacy*, 117.

4. Barrie Gunter and Rachel Vinney, *Seeing is Believing: Religion and Television in the 1990s* (London: John Libbey/Independent Television Commission, 1994), 32.

5. Mass Observation, *Puzzled People* (London: Gollanz, 1948), 32.

6. David Hay and Ann Morisy, 'Reports of Ecstatic, Paranormal or Religious Experience in Great Britain and the United States: a Comparison of Trends', *Journal for the Scientific Study of Religion*, 17 (1978), 255. It is worth noting that Hay and Morisy's data show a very strong connection between conventional indices of religiosity and the experiences they document and measure, which hardly supports the general claim that 'implicit' religion is an alternative to, and compensation for the absence of, conventional religion. Bibby tried and failed to find evidence of 'implicit religion' in Canadian survey data. He concluded that 'lack of empirically identifiable invisible religion is further evident in the answers posed to the so-called ultimate questions. Only the theme of traditional religious commitment is consistently associated with clear-cut answers to such questions' (Reginald Bibby, 'Searching for Invisible Thread: Meaning Systems in Contemporary Canada', *Journal for the Scientific Study of Religion*, 22 (1983), 117).

7. Obelkevitch, quoted by David Hempton, 'Religious Life in Industrial Britain', in Sheridan Gilley and W. J. Sheils (eds.), *A History of Religion in Britain: Practice and Belief from Pre-Roman Times to the Present* (Oxford: Blackwell, 1994), 310.

8. Gunter and Vinney, *Seeing is Believing*, 53.

9. Ibid. 51.

Notes to Chapter Three

1. Ben Bradley, 'UK Jews Fight Dwindling Faith', *Independent on Sunday*, 1 May 1994.

2. Iain McRobert, 'The New Black-Led Pentecostal Church in Britain', in Paul Badham (ed.), *Religion, State and Society in Modern Britain* (Lampeter: Edwin Mellen, 1989), 127.

3. Ken Pryce, *Endless Pressure: A Study of West Indian Life-Styles in Bristol* (Harmondsworth, Middx.: Penguin, 1979), 221.

4. Ibid. 214.

5. Jorgen Nielsen, *Muslims in Western Europe* (Edinburgh: Edinburgh University Press, 1992), 42.

6. Malise Ruthven, *A Satanic Affair: Salman Rushdie and the Rage of Islam* (London: Chatto and Windus, 1990).

7. W. Owen Cole, 'Sikhs in Britain', in Badham (ed.), *Religion, State and Society*, 265.

Notes to Chapter Four

1. Roy Wallis, *The Elementary Forms of the New Religious Life* (London: Routledge & Kegan Paul, 1984), 28.
2. Peter Brierley, *The New Age is Coming!* (London: Research Monograph 35; MARC Europe, 1991), summarizes the frequency tables from the project.
3. William Bloom, *The New Age* (London: Rider, 1991), p. xvi.
4. Ibid., p. xvii.
5. Ibid.
6. J. Gordon Melton, Jerome Clark, and Aidan A. Kelly, *New Age Almanac* (New York: Visible Ink, 1991), 96–7.
7. Carol Riddell, *The Findhorn Community: Creating a Human Identity for the 21st Century* (Findhorn, Forres, Moray: Findhorn Press, 1990), 15.
8. Eileen Caddy and Liza Hollingshead, *Flight into Freedom: The Autobiography of the Co-Founder of the Findhorn Community* (Longmead, Dorset: Element Books, 1988), 87.
9. Jeremy Slocombe and Eve Ward, 'Willing to Change: An Interview with Eileen Caddy', *One World: The Findhorn Foundation and Community Magazine*, 12 (winter 1993–4), 9.
10. Melton, Clark, and Kelly, *New Age Almanac*, 40.
11. Hans H. Gerth and C. Wright Mills, *From Max Weber: Essays in Sociology* (London: Routledge, 1970), 51.
12. Bryan Wilson, 'The Functions of Religion: A Reappraisal', *Religion*, 18 (1988), 207.
13. James M. Martin, *Actualizations: Beyond est* (San Francisco: San Francisco Book Co., 1977), 55.
14. Philip Rieff, *The Triumph of the Therapeutic* (Harmondsworth, Middx.: Penguin, 1973), 224.
15. Jeremy Slocombe, 'Last Thoughts', *One Earth*, 14 (summer 1994), 19.
16. *Good Housekeeping* (Oct. 1993).

Notes to Chapter Five

1. Bryan Wilson, *Religion in Sociological Perspective* (Oxford: Oxford University Press, 1982), 154.

Index

Index